14-

W9-BJJ-263

*Love
and
Discipline*

Love
and
Discipline

Prepared by the
Bank Street College
of
Education

Barbara Brenner
Author

Leah Levinger, Ph.D.
Consultant

William H. Hooks
Series Editor

BALLANTINE BOOKS • NEW YORK

Cover design: Andrew M. Newman
Cover photo: Peterson/T.I.B.

Library of Congress Catalog Card Number: 82-90851
ISBN: 0-345-31147-7 (hdcvr)
ISBN: 0-345-30520-5 (pbk)
Manufactured in the United States of America
First Edition: April 1983
10 9 8 7 6 5 4 3 2 1

Contents

Expanded Contents

CHAPTER 4
Threes, Fours, Fives

55

CHAPTER 5
School Discipline

Words and discipline are both tricky. A word may have a very different meaning in one situation from what it does in another.

Take the word "power." Power can be considered a bad—even a vicious—thing when it stands for the ruthless, forceful domination of one individual over another, whether parent and child, teacher and student, master and slave, or bully and scapegoat. Yet power is also often a very laudatory term, as when we speak of "a powerful thinker" or "a powerful runner" or "a powerful pianist," where what we mean is a vigorous and dedicated expression of a skill and a craft.

In the same way, "control" can be a negative or a positive term. It's negative when it means domination, bossiness, and lack of respect for another person. It's also negative when it means a person is "overly controlled," locked into feelings and unable to express them, inhibited and unable to be spontaneous. Yet control in the use of one's body in athletics or dance or carpentry or other physical expression, control in any of the arts or intellectual pursuits, is thought of as a very valuable quality.

"Discipline" shares much in common with these two terms. Many people who have sought freedom and spontaneity see discipline as an expression of old-fashioned stodginess at best, or harshness and stifling of spontaneity and even downright cruelty at worst. But "self-discipline" is considered an admirable quality. It's an attribute needed to attain mastery over one's body so it is free to do what one wants it to do in athletics or acting or dancing. It is also associated with mastery in a field such as music or mathematics or typing. And it can even make possible mastery of one's emotions so that one is free to express love and able to control anger.

Keeping life in order so one is free to spend time and energy doing what one likes to do is ultimately what discipline is all about. Part of keeping life in order is to be disciplined about time so one does one's work, enjoys doing it, gets it done, and is free to play. Discipline in relations with other people may ultimately boil down to respecting their desires as much as one's own. When discipline is in place, one need not waste energy with ruckuses and fights and competitions, but is free to love others, work collaboratively, and have fun.

In this book Barbara Brenner makes a significant contribution to our understanding of discipline, while having the gift of writing in simple language about everyday life. This is because she genuinely believes that people's own experiences matter, and that all people are different. While that sounds like the basis for any kind of book of advice to parents about child rearing, it's actually quite rare in this field. Far too often educators have an inflated ideal of what a parent ought to be like and a prescriptive "this way is best" approach to child rearing. Along with rigidity and oversimplifying comes the view that all children are alike, that three-year-olds are all able to behave and understand in a certain way, four-year-olds in a more advanced way, and so on. But Brenner is able to take seriously the idea of individual difference on the part of both parents and child. Hence, she does not give "advice" which must be unerringly, implicitly followed. Rather, she provokes people to reexamine themselves and their own values and experiences, and also to look very closely at what kind of children they have in terms of temperament. Brenner's ultimate aim is to be of use to parents in their own discovery of what will work best for their particular child. This includes recognition of the ultimate goals they have. It also demands that the parents think through what is possible and wished for and where they can be most themselves instead of aiming for any artificial and unreachable ideal.

Brenner is able to use the thinking of a variety of scholars, educators, and therapists who have, over the past fifty years, clarified and articulated many concepts about the development of children. She emphasizes material that has come from three major sources: the practical reinforcement approach, Freud's psychoanalytic work, and Piaget's studies on how children grow and learn.

The practical reinforcement concept maintains that a child, like a dog, a horse, or most domesticated animals (cats excepted!), is able to learn the ways of a household by a series of repeated rewards (positive reinforcements) and punishments (negative reinforcements). The emphasis in this point of view is on action—repetitive, intense reinforcements so that a child learns almost automatically how to respond. There are certain situations where this seemingly mechanistic way of working is useful, such as preventing physical harm when the child first becomes mobile. With negative and positive reinforcements, the toddler can be automatically restrained from grabbing sharp objects, turning on the stove, or thrusting little hands into boiling water. Outside, the youngster will learn to refrain from running into the street where there is traffic or racing up to hug a strange large dog. But even this kind of training, in order to ensure the child's physical survival, may be worth another look. While children may not have the adult language to explain why something is allowed and something else is prohibited, they pick up quite early feelings of fear or disgust or panic from the adult who is administering the reinforcement. The method of reinforcement has to recognize the differences of what will work at what ages or with a particular child. For example, is there any way that a ten- or twelve-month-old infant can be "trained" to eat in a tidy, mannerly fashion?

A second body of knowledge and theory about children incorporated here comes from the work of Sigmund Freud and many doctors, educators, pediatricians, and psychologists who have followed him. In this approach, there is more emphasis on how individuals feel. Not only are the feelings of adults important, but the feelings of children, even infants, are important as well. Further, people may have feelings that influence their behavior, but may not be aware of them. Great changes occurred in our way of regarding ourselves when this part of Freud's thinking became recognized and accepted. This resulted in new directions in the rearing and education of children. We also have come to recognize that children respond to situations in complicated ways that reach back to their earliest training. For instance, when presented with a new task, a seven-year-old may rely on something that started five years before, when he was a toddler, and received cuddling, nuzzling, and chuckling approval that gave him an ongoing feeling of confidence which he has drawn upon ever since. One could also choose examples of the opposite effects of painful or frightening or demeaning or humiliating experiences from far, far back that make for a particular viewpoint about oneself.

What Brenner so well recognizes is that it is not always one act or attitude on the part of parents that influences child feelings and, hence, behavior, but a combination of many things.

Finally, there is Freud's important recognition that people very often have not only differing but conflicting feelings about the same thing. They may be aware of only one of these feelings. But both are present. And the one they are not aware of may very often negate or at least obstruct their way of trying to carry out the other feeling. Brenner is clearly aware that parents, sincerely trying to do a good job in the rearing of their children, may be hampered by the unspoken and unrecognized early experiences they themselves had as children. They may be burdened by concerns about the way the neighbors, the children's teachers, or other adults will be judging them. This sense of being judged may hang over a parent and stand in the way of his or her being able to carry out deeply felt child-raising beliefs and principles.

Jean Piaget is another scholar and explorer of human development who has given our current generation deeper understanding of the way children grow and learn. His emphasis was on the way children develop their understanding of the world and the manner in which they think. He delineated—through a number of very carefully detailed studies—the way that growth occurs in the child's understanding of the physical universe, cause and effect, language, numbers, and the social-moral climate. In all of these areas, Piaget has helped us see that each child moves at his own rate, aided by a favorable, stimulating, and emotionally accepting life situation, but always with some kind of inner time clock.

This understanding has been enormously useful to educators and parents. They have come to recognize that children differ from adults and adolescents not only in how much they know but also in what they know and how they reason and come to conclusions. The importance of direct physical demonstration or experience of the physical world may, in the earliest part of life, be of greater meaning for the child than language. Even when the child can talk glibly about the tyrannosaurus, stegosaurus, and other dinosaurs, he may not, for example, have any concept of time; not just the time frame of dinosaurs, but how it is that a grandfather is older than a father who is older than the son. In the same way, a child can learn mechanically not to do something because he'll be punished for it. But the difference between right and wrong and an understanding of how his or her actions will affect other people and their happiness are far more mature concepts; a child will have to grow awhile to be ready to comprehend them, no matter what teaching and example are present.

Throughout this book, Brenner is able to take these three different approaches and weave them together or to stress one or the other when it is most useful. She sees the child as a constantly growing and changing person, always in continuity with his previous experiences and his particular temperament. He is not just acted upon by the adults in his environment but is able to meet them halfway, able—at a certain point in his life—to take in and understand certain ideas and screen out others that are still too complex for him. Also, because of who he is at a given point, he influences the people around him who then, in a chain reaction, respond to him in a different way. This interaction of the child's own inner growth and relation with the environment, and also between his feelings and his thoughts, is a major theme of this book.

How you as a parent use this book is, of course, up to you. You can read it through quite easily, because it is so vividly and clearly written. You can look up various parts that may give you a specific answer for a specific problem or situation. Ideally, however, you should read it and think about it slowly, at various stages in your child's and in your own growth. It is designed to be a springboard for your own thinking. It can help you experiment as you respond to the complexities of your child and your growing up together in today's world.

Leah Levinger, Ph.D.

Acknowledgments

Grateful acknowledgment is made to Joëlle Delbourgo for her role in conceptualizing this series; to Pat Ayres for bringing Bank Street and Ballantine Books together; to Dr. Richard Ruopp, president of Bank Street College, and to the faculty who supported us in this venture; and to Mary Fitzpatrick for manuscript preparation.

Love
and
Discipline

Chapter 1

Parents and Kids and Discipline

You parents all that children have,
And you that have got none,
If you would have them safe abroad,
First keep them well at home.

The Real Meaning of Discipline

Discipline. We all know children should have it. At the same time, we're uneasy. Because *discipline* has gotten to be a buzz word that doesn't tell us what it is so much as how it makes us feel. And how it makes us feel is uncomfortable. Invoking discipline conjures up punishment and denial of pleasure. On the other hand, the idea of *no* discipline produces a picture of sloppiness, backtalk, poor grades, and worse. Either way, we don't like it.

Too bad such a sound idea has gotten such a bad name. Maybe it's high time we restored discipline's tarnished image and swung back to some of its original, positive meaning. Like this simple definition:

> DISCIPLINE: Training that molds character and orderly thought and action.

Does Everyone Need Discipline?

Yes! Some things come naturally to humans. Children progress from lying to sitting to standing to walking through a process of maturation that requires very little help from us parents. But other aspects of growing up require some training. For example, every human being has to learn restraint. We learn from parents and siblings, and later from others what kind of behavior is permitted in our society and what's beyond the bounds. We learn what's dangerous and what's safe, what we can dare and what brings censure. We learn how to do things, how to organize time and energy into tasks that are important to our personal survival and, later,

1

to our satisfaction in our adult lives. And we also learn social responsibility, our obligation to the family and to the larger group. We learn caring. In a sense, we learn all these things through discipline.

Imagine if there were no boundaries. A race of strange creatures would roam the world, unable to cope with the most elemental dangers, unable to manage even the most rudimentary tasks, and unable to relate to other people on any but the most brutal level.

Discipline is basic. To deprive a child of discipline is to take away coping skills, to impair selfhood, and to render the individual a freak and an outcast in the human community.

Children learn the ways of the world and their place in it by a constant process of trying things and by being limited, restrained, reinforced, and redirected—in other words, by being disciplined. It's a slow process. Sometimes it can be quite painful for both parent and child. And difficult. But it's absolutely vital.

Does Discipline Kill Individuality?

One of the charges sometimes leveled against effective discipline is that it kills creativity and individuality. Is that true? Does applying the brakes to "free expression" make Jack a dull boy? Does abiding by firm rules cripple Jill's ego and lock her in? There's no evidence of it. Quite the contrary. In every study that has been done, well-adjusted and achieving youngsters seem to come from homes where there are clear rules and standards—firm discipline, offered with love. People raised in this atmosphere acquire the self-discipline to master their craft or profession (often, interestingly, called a discipline) and to order their lives for maximum contentment, productivity, and originality.

Where Does Discipline Come From?

Discipline isn't some artificial invention. It comes from the inside out. We use it even when we don't realize it. But *how* we use discipline, what we say and do, is highly individual.

Most of the rules we use we got from our parents. It used to be that these rules were passed down from generation to generation pretty intact. Parents accepted without much question that what had been good enough for them would be good enough for *their* children. The apple didn't fall far from the tree because family members were all pretty much the same variety of "apple."

But things changed. People began to move around more. Families were not as close. The roots of generations were disturbed and the young "transplants" had to grow up under conditions very different from the ones under which their parents had grown. There were new influences—cars, industrial inventions. Sometimes there was a whole new country and language to adjust to. There came a time when the rules that had worked for our grandparents and parents didn't seem to cover all the situations that the next generation faced. New parents were no longer willing to accept the old ways as the only ways.

This dramatic shift in child-rearing styles turned out to be both good and bad. The good part was that the new generation was freed to try new ways of raising children. It was more open to new ideas and not afraid to break with the past, sometimes with marvelous results.

The bad part was that we parents were often confused. In dumping some of the old, outmoded ideas, a vacuum was left. And a host of fashions in discipline poured into it. They went in and out of style like skirt lengths, leaving us with one set of "musts" for a first child and a new set for the second. In an effort to follow the latest trend, mothers and fathers sometimes abandoned or denied their own best instincts and gut feelings. They lost sight of the most basic, commonsense rules.

A New Discipline

All of this was bound to create a backlash. Today many people, disturbed with the results of the "new ways," want to return to what they call "good, old-fashioned discipline." They want an end to all the experimenting, the trial and error. They want to go back to what they see as discipline that is proven and reliable. Who can blame them?

The trouble is, we can't go back. Some of the old ways don't work anymore, partly because we live in a world of accelerated change on every front. For example, just a generation ago, most women stayed home and reared their children. Today most women work. Many children are in day care or with a housekeeper. In addition, there are many more single-parent households. Nowadays, *who* does the disciplining is as much a subject as the discipline itself.

And we can't ignore the many new discoveries in child development that have taken place in the last twenty-five years. We certainly can't throw away everything new that we've learned, just as we can't reject everything that is older and more traditional. What we should do is retain the soundest ideas from the past and merge them with the best and most functional newer ideas, keeping in mind shifting family patterns and differing family styles. What are some of these styles?

Styles of Discipline

Studies have shown that discipliners fall roughly into three groups: *authoritarian, permissive,* and *authoritative.*

Jim and Peggy Snead are examples of authoritarian parents. They represent the strictest end of the discipline spectrum. Both Peggy and Jim insist that their kids "toe the line." The children wipe their feet before they come in the house or else! They also do chores, say "please" and "thank you," mind their table manners and submit to a homework check every night. They get spanked when they're "bad" (Jim and Peggy's term). Jim says, "We keep the kids on a tight rein, but we think it's necessary. Spare the rod and spoil the child is our motto, but as the kids get older we're finding it more difficult to keep them in check." The fact that Jim speaks of keeping his kids "in check" is a clue to their philosophy, which is one of *control.*

Nelda and Jay Moran represent a totally opposite view. Nelda's parents were very strict, and she is determined not to bring her kids up that way. As a result, she swung around 180 degrees to become a permissive parent. The Moran children are brought up with very few "dos" and "don'ts." They eat when and if they feel like it, and are never instructed about manners or morals. They aren't required to clean their rooms or help in the house. And they always feel free to express themselves, sometimes in terms that shock even their parents. Nelda half-apologetically laughs, "They're great kids to exchange ideas with, but don't invite them to dinner." As Jim and Peggy stress *controlling* their children, Nelda and Jay seem to believe in almost total *freedom.*

Doris and Hy Bryant fall somewhere between these two extremes. They expect certain things from their children, but try to gear their expectations to the child's capabilities (small expectations for small children). They make it a point to give reasons for the rules and limits they set down and don't expect blind obedience to everything. There is talk of manners and morals in this house. Hy confesses that he loses his temper from time to time and "swats" one of the kids, but on the whole the children are disciplined through reason and discussion.

The Bryants are authoritative parents. They exert their authority, but are not nearly as rigid and dictatorial as the authoritarian Jim and Peggy. Nor do they give in as much as the permissive Nelda and Jay.

Most American parents fall into this authoritative, or middle-of-the-road category. Interestingly enough, studies have shown that the largest number of well-adjusted, achieving youngsters come from this group. Which may be a way of saying that somewhere between being "tough" and "easy" with your offspring is the place to be.

Kid Styles

Just as parents can be roughly divided into three discipline groups (authoritative, authoritarian, permissive), kids can be seen as falling into three basic categories: *easy, slow to warm up, difficult.*

It appears that some of the tendencies to be one way or the other are inborn. Others develop as a result of how the environment acts on these inborn tendencies. So what kind of Jack or Joan you eventually wind up with seems to be a complicated mix of how Jack or Joan is born and what happens to him or her afterward. Looked at this way, you can understand how an "easy" baby may set the stage almost immediately for the treatment that is likely to continue to bring out easiness and good nature. On the other hand, a child born "difficult" can become more or less difficult depending on how its caretakers interact with it.

What seems clear is that a baby isn't simply a blank sheet on which life can write, but an organism that comes into the world with some equipment of its own. Surprisingly, even looks have something to do with a baby's future. Large, good-looking babies please their parents more than small, undersized ones and may affect the way their mothers and fathers treat them. It may not be fair, but it's a fact, and parents should be aware of it. It's a good idea for all of us to examine our values in this respect and not have unrealistic expectations for our kids. New insights could lead to changes in behavior that might make all the difference to a child.

Considering all the elements, raising each of your children may be a little like making a stew. You start with some basic ingredients and a general "recipe." But then you always add your own personal touches. And every time you add something you change the flavor. The final dish is the result of many things, including more than a dash of experimentation, a sensitivity to what you're cooking up, and a fair dollop of guesswork.

The Middle Road

We lean toward the middle-of-the-road approach. We stand somewhere between the toughies and the softies in discipline. But even if you are philosophically committed to one of the two end positions, you may find material here that will help you. If you're a strict parent, you may find in reading this book that you can achieve some of the same results without coming down quite so hard on your kids. If you're a permissive parent, we may be able to show you how to achieve freedom without anarchy.

And if you're a middle-of-the-roader, we'll give you specific suggestions as to how you can implement what you believe in.

Oh, Dad, Poor Dad

It's only recently that many fathers have begun to take a rightful place alongside mothers as co-nurturers rather than simply as enforcers. Traditionally, dad's role was to mete out discipline, especially punishment. "Just wait until I tell your father" was guaranteed to strike terror into the hearts of misbehavers. And implicit in the words was that dad was a wrathful ogre. It was a pretty heavy (and unfair) image for the male half of the parenting team to carry around.

Fortunately, many dads are now discovering the joys of being involved with the loving and caring aspects of parenting. They're learning that they, too, are entitled to hug and cuddle as well as holler and spank. Dads are beginning to realize that it's not only fair for them to take over some of the nurturing, but that it's fun. And both mom and dad are becoming aware that to assign narrowly defined roles to either parent (moms feed, clothe, and sing lullabies; dads play baseball, give advice, and discipline) cheats both parent and child.

Discipline and Child Development

As soon as any infant is born, *patterns* of interaction are set up between parents and child. As your infant grows and you deal with more and more complex behavior, successful later disciplines are built on some of these original "imprints." So obviously, one of the important things you can do is set up sensible beginning patterns and then follow through in an orderly way.

We think the best guide to follow-through discipline is to begin it in the cradle and work hand in hand with the youngster's own development. Which is why, in the following chapters, you'll read about the behavior you can expect at a certain age, before you read what to do about it.

Here's a rough outline of the various stages in discipline, based on child development guidelines.

Infant Discipline

A time to establish patterns of *love, trust,* and *security,* along with a comforting sense of *order* and *routine.* This is also the time baby develops the beginnings of a *sense of self.*

Toddler Discipline

A time to help the child to conform to important rules of *safety* while encouraging growing *independence.* Toddlerhood is the time discipline should limit *aggression,* help a youngster cope with *frustration,* and reinforce a sense of self while setting firm *limits.*

Preschool Discipline

Parents need to help youngsters *interpret* the world. They should guide *coping* and *social skills, attending* and *learn-*

ing, and begin to help a child acquire *values* and *moral standards.*

Middle-Years Discipline

Children need continuous reinforcement of all the previously learned disciplines. In addition, they need guidance in *decision-making,* in *work habits,* in *friendship* and other *value systems.* Middle-years children need family discussion about moral questions, such as frank talk about *sex* and *drugs* (including alcohol, cigarettes, and even coffee).

Adolescent Discipline

A look ahead with the emphasis on providing *consistency* with the ultimate goal of self-discipline and independence for the young person; looking toward a happy, productive, and decent adulthood.

Different Strokes

Discipline, however, isn't a hard and fast set of rules that will work with any child. You can't only know *what* to do. You have to know *whom* you're working with. Some children can be told "no" once and that will be it for life. Other kids need more guidance and insistence. Children vary in their responses to discipline. Firm tones can bring tears to the eyes of Sam, where yelling will roll off Terry's back. So you can't come on in the same way to sensitive Sam as you do to tough-minded Terry.

The different strokes may be cultural, too. Anyone who has traveled is bound to be struck with the varying styles of bringing up children that you see in different countries. These cultural patterns may persist here in the "melting pot," which means that parents in a Chinese neighborhood, or in a Spanish area, may have notions of discipline quite different from yours. It's sometimes useful to take a look at other people's ways and learn from them. It's also a good idea to look at your own ethnic or cultural roots and see if there aren't some things in your background that are worth using in the bringing up of your children.

Parents and Discipline

Parents as Models

Discipline is for parents as well as for children. What you do is as crucial as what you say. Kids pick up all kinds of cues from their parents. It's simple: If you want neatness, you've got to be neat yourself. If you don't want your child to lie, you have to tell the truth. In a sense, what *they* see is what *you* get. Which doesn't mean that you always have to be perfect. In fact, perfection can be quite a burden for your offspring! But if your child views you as being, on balance, a good person, he or she is apt to be quite tolerant of shortcomings. "My mother has a short fuse," says Jed, philosophically. "But she never stays mad. And if she loses her temper at me for something that isn't my fault, she apologizes after she has calmed down. She's nice that way."

How Many Parents?

Discipline today also has to take into account the changes in marital patterns. Many children of today have only one parent. Others shuttle back and forth between two households. And some live in situations with stepsisters and stepbrothers, or with half brothers and sisters who may have been raised in a different way.

These new circumstances may make problems for both the parents and children involved. There are no easy answers to the dilemmas that arise in single-parent or multiple families.

Single parents have it hardest because all the discipline decisions are up to them. They often have no one with whom to share child care. Mother or, in some cases, dad, must always be the enforcer, disciplinarian, "bad guy." It's not the most pleasant job and it's no wonder that single parents have doubts about what they're doing. Sometimes the doubts cause them problems. Youngsters sense this and either feel insecure or try to take advantage.

Sometimes a divorced parent will try to undermine the custodial parent. It's hard for discipline to work against this boring from within. Divorced partners should try to come to agreement on discipline, for the child's sake.

"Two-family" households are even more complicated. If

you're a step-parent, your spouse's child may not accept your discipline readily. You may not approve of the way your stepson or stepdaughter was raised before you came into the picture. But you may have to live with some of the results. And before you try to change the rules, you should see whether everyone in your new family approves of the changes. To be evenhanded, discipline has to apply equally to yours, his, and, eventually, to both of yours.

Child or Children?

One of the factors that affects discipline in a family is simply numbers. Obviously, the parents of one child or two can devote more time to the fine points of discipline than the parents of many. As one harassed mother of five said, "I have enough trouble getting everyone into boots and snow-suits, without getting into each kid's psyche."

But discipline is important for the parents of a "passel" of kids. The household of many personalities and age groups needs the orderliness and organization that discipline can provide. You may not be able to give each child the concentration of attention that the only child gets, but you can give each kid equal time.

Some large families may decide, sensibly, that they have to run a tighter ship than small families do. You may find this is true. Everyone in a large family has to cooperate and follow basic family rules; otherwise, there's chaos. Surprisingly, kids respond well to this clear need for cooperation. Older siblings learn to help younger ones. No one resents chores if everyone has them. There's no reason why children in large families should be any less disciplined than children in small families.

Consistency

One of the foundation rocks of discipline is consistency. You shouldn't say one thing and do another. You can't make a hard and fast rule one time and then let it slide another time. If you want your discipline to work, you have to pretty much decide where you stand on important issues, and then *stand* there.

That's one kind of consistency, the consistency of hewing to your own line. But what about consistency of discipline among all the people who deal with your child? Can one be strict and one soft? How about permissive parent and authoritarian nursemaid? Not good. Among the people who share the caring for your child, everyone should see eye to eye.

How do you achieve this desirable unanimity? By talking it over. There's nothing wrong with having a summit conference with your spouse on the subject of child rearing. Include the housekeeper or grandpa or Aunt Rose if any of them are involved in the day-to-day care of your offspring. Decide on a general plan. Then—everybody should stick to it. There's nothing more confusing to a small child than a different set of rules from each grown-up who takes care of him. On the other hand, when he gets older he will be able to handle with greater ease the mixed values of, say, a parent and a teacher.

Discipline: Boys vs. Girls

What are little boys made of?
What are little boys made of?
Frogs and snails and puppy dogs' tails
That's what little boys are made of.

What are little girls made of?
What are little girls made of?
Sugar and spice and everything nice
That's what little girls are made of.

The little nursery rhyme above was written a long time ago by an anonymous author. Obviously, Anonymous was on to something about how people look on girl children versus boy children.

In this case, girls are perceived as being nicer. But the discrimination could just as easily be reversed. In many cultures, boys are the preferred sex. In not-so-ancient China, this was carried to an extreme; girl children were often drowned. And when the longed-for event of a male birth occurred, the parents were at pains to conceal it from vengeful gods. They wailed and muttered "Miserable girl" just to throw the powers off the track!

In modern times, few parents come out and say "miserable girl." But they may feel more favorably disposed toward a boy. More often, favoritism takes the form of a different set of aspirations for girls and boys. These unequal attitudes have a profound effect on discipline.

They may begin in the cradle. Listen to this conversation at cribside:

"Isn't she sweet? And so good. She's a real little lady already."

"Aren't you lucky she's a girl? They're so much easier to handle."

Now let's take a peek around the boy's bassinet:

"Listen to him holler! He's a real tough guy already."

"He knows what he wants. He's not going to let anyone push him around."

So it goes. We set up patterns of what we expect and what we want.

We expect girls to be:

- gentle and quiet
- neat and clean
- helpful and cooperative
- good in school
- loving and affectionate

We expect boys to be:

- loud and boisterous
- good at sports and rough games
- slow to mature
- less able to sit quietly
- more trouble in school

Clearly, some of these traits may be true for an individual boy or girl. They may even be true for a sizable majority of the group. But what we don't know is whether these traits are inborn or are there because we treat boys and girls differently. In any case, we shouldn't be surprised when we get the behavior we anticipated. Many studies have shown that children behave the way they're expected to behave.

No one is quicker to pick up on double standards in discipline than the children themselves. Each sex tends to see it as the other one getting the better deal:

"My brother doesn't have to help around the house nearly as much as I do."

"The teacher picks on all the boys and dotes on all the girls."

"My father hits me all the time. He never lays a finger on my sister, and she does worse things than I do."

Some kids can see unfairness even when it's not directed at them:

"I got all the breaks. My sister was treated like a second-class citizen."

"When I used to hit my brother, my mother would say to him, 'Don't hit her back. She's a girl.'"

Many of these attitudes we're not even aware of. The parent who shakes his head and says, "Our Joan is so easy, but that Jack—what a wild Indian!" may actually be bragging. Having a wild boy may satisfy our "macho" sense. Having a quiet boy or a boy who is not interested in wild play may be thought by some parents to be "sissy." And the girl who is wild and rambunctious may not fit into family standards for daughters.

Whether you expect more or less from your boy child, whether you spare the rod with Joan or Jack, chances are it's part of the ways you grew up with. Nevertheless, it's worth it to rethink some of these prejudices, for the sake of good discipline. Try to figure out why the bad guy is always a guy, or why "goody two shoes" always seems to be a girl. Both boys and girls need to feel that they're good when they are. Both boys and girls need firm discipline when they're not. When you dish up the discipline, you need to ladle it out in equal portions.

The Limits of Discipline

In the developmental sense, all the world's a stage. Your youngster will probably go through every one. And the best disciplinary strategy isn't going to work with your kids 100 percent of the time. Your toddler, restrained from biting, may rise to bite again. Don't worry; someday she will know better. And maybe you weren't able to instill in your young musician a passion for the discipline of practicing on the piano. But maybe you instilled a love of music. Win a few, lose a few. The important thing is to hang in there with the kind of training you believe in.

Punishment

But no discipline works all the time. And when it doesn't, you have to try a mixture of strategies. You'll run across many of them in this book: distracting, negotiating, ignoring, even punishing when the necessity arises. No one strategy can be expected to work every time, or with every age.

Punishment is going to come up from time to time. No parent enjoys punishing a child, but it is often an effective means of enforcing rules or making "the consequences" real.

Some parents believe in talk rather than punishment. Talk is great, if the child is able to understand what you're saying. And *if* the way you say it isn't so hurtful that it masks your message.

Can you compare talking to hitting? Talking is usually better. But as a sign at Bank Street School poignantly declares, "Sticks and stones can break your bones, but words can break your heart." Sarcasm, ridicule, nagging, are all punishments that can leave scars. They are "wipe-out" techniques that can do more damage than the behavior they're designed to prevent.

Language and Discipline

There's much more to language than meets the ear. It's not only what you say but what you don't say. And it's not only the content, it's the tone. You can see this clearly if you talk to a puppy. You can say to it, "My, but you're a dumb mutt." If you say it with a smile and a loving tone, the puppy will wag its tail with joy. Same thing goes for your toddler. If you coo, "What a slob you are," your child will hear affection in your voice and grin at you through a face full of tomato sauce.

What about silence? Is it golden? Only sometimes. Other times it can be a devastating form of discipline, much worse than speaking hard truths. There's a good reason why solitary confinement is considered an extreme form of criminal punishment, and why the silent treatment has been used as a form of torture. Looked at this way, you have to reject both protracted silence and solitude as punishments used long-term against kids.

Spanking

> If I had a donkey that wouldn't go,
> Would I beat him? Oh no, no.

If all else fails, what about spanking?

Does it really help? Or is it part of the problem instead of part of the solution?

An occasional slap on the backside (never the face) may say what you want to say and be very effective. The big trouble with hitting is that it signals that all other channels of communication have broken down and that this is the only thing you felt would reach the child. I always felt like a failure when I hit my kids, and I personally don't recommend it as a way of disciplining. Not many people really are in favor of spanking. Most educators think it is very damaging to hit small children. Most parents who spank feel guilty about it afterward and may remember it long after the child has forgotten. Here are two views of spanking, this one from an eight-year-old:

> If I do something wrong, I'd rather have my mother give me a smack and get it over with. Sometimes, instead of spanking me, she doesn't speak to me for a whole day. That's the worst. I feel like I'll never earn her love again. I hate feeling bad for so long.

A father has this to say on the subject:

> It's not worth it to spank. I used to get my temper tantrum over with, but I found I hadn't taught Phillip a thing. The worst part of it was that there was an escalator clause. I was beginning to hit harder and harder to get my message across. One day I realized that soon it wouldn't be spanking, but something worse.

Child Abuse

Child abuse is the ugliest face that discipline can wear. Ugly as it is, it's worth bringing out of the closet because there's a lot of it around. And it's not only in poor homes, broken homes, and among people who are freaks. Children can be abused by otherwise "normal" people. The same impulse that causes a pet owner to kick his dog can unleash unreasoning rage against a small child at the end of a long, trying day.

We all have our moments—when we're pestered beyond our limits or embarrassed by a misbehaving child, or at our wit's end because of a youngster's contrariness. This is the time when parents have to be disciplined themselves. Maybe they need to go into isolation for a while to cool off (the same treatment they've given the kids). Or maybe it's time for the other parent to take over. In any case, all parents need, in these moments, to practice the restraint they're trying to teach.

What if you can't? There's a question every parent should face honestly.

If you have a nagging suspicion that you're hitting too often or too hard, or if you have a gut feeling that you are running out of control when you discipline, you should call your local community group on child abuse and talk about it. The people there will be sympathetic to your problem. You *will* get help. It's no disgrace to need support and to seek it. The disgrace is to keep child abuse in the closet.

Remember, children are mimics. The abused child grows up to abuse. As Eda LeShan says in her book *The Roots of Crime,* "The majority of people who commit serious crimes were battered and abused children. By the time they were five or six years old they were sure they were 'no good' and deserved to be punished."

Kids Talk about Discipline

Not Enough

What do kids have to say about discipline? They all hate it, right? Wrong. When children are polled, most of them come up voting for parents who lay down the law and give them rules. One young adult, looking back, expressed it this way:

> My parents let me do pretty much what I wanted and very seldom disciplined me. I thought they really didn't care about me because they gave me so few rules and restrictions.

"There weren't many walls to push down," says another young woman who grew up in the sixties. There is regret in the tone of both these statements. It's as if these young people wanted something from their parents that they didn't get. There seems to be an almost universal longing among children for some clear limits within which to operate, for some boundaries against which to push. This feeling was expressed most perceptively by a twelve-year-old who told her mother, "My job is to get away with as much as I can and your job is to stop me."

Too Much

On the other hand, there are the voices of children who had too much discipline. Some of them express themselves in late-blooming revolt against all constraints. A few are heard from in adulthood on the psychiatrist's couch. Joan Crawford's daughter is a particularly eloquent voice for children who have been dealt with too harshly. Unfortunately, some of the testimony from the most harshly disciplined children comes from behind prison walls.

Asked what they disliked most about parental discipline, most kids didn't say physical punishment. They said what they hated was being told, or made to feel, that they were "bad." It was clear that the kids were talking here about situations where they were left with no sense of self-worth. They could handle discipline that said they were wrong about something specific, but not discipline that wiped out their feelings of self-esteem.

Fairness

The other thing that children spoke a lot about was fairness. Fairness seemed to figure quite high on their totem pole of values. They would accept, for instance, a pretty stern rebuke over something that was clearly a family rule. On the other hand, they thought punishment was unfair if they were given no chance to explain or if they had not known in advance that what they did was wrong.

You and This Book

By now it must be clear that good discipline isn't something that just happens. Parents have to try for it in a conscious way. The fact that you are reading this book is an indication that you are interested in finding ways to discipline that will square with your notions of child rearing. You will find them in the following pages.

What you won't find are many exact "recipes," and for a good reason. I can suggest some general guidelines, but the rest of the essential ingredients are ones you'll have to supply. They'll come out of the dynamics of your particular family.

Effective discipline has to take into account not only what you are like, but also what you value. More than that, it has to be tailored to each of those unique individuals who are your children. It's an exciting idea, the realization that we share certain basics but are all different. Dealing with those differences is both the fun and the challenge of raising children.

That's why there are some things you'll read here that you'll want to try and some that you won't. For the same reason, some of the ideas will work for you and some won't. Some strategies may be just the ticket for one of your kids but not for the others. And you'll find, as you go through the chapters, that you'll have your own order of priorities. You may skip some behaviors and then find that they crop up later. Some of the case histories may sound exactly like they were written about your Jack or Joan, while others may seem entirely alien. Whether you eventually get to use part or all of the information doesn't matter. What is comforting to know is that behavior can change. You yourself can change. And so can your children. The other reassuring news is that the family, far from being obsolete, is still the single most influential force in a child's life. That means parents count. So stand up and be counted!

Chapter 2
Patterning Baby

*A Nursery Rhyme
(with options)*

*There was an old lady
Who lived in a shoe.
She had so many children
She didn't know what to do.
She fed them all broth
Without any bread;
She spanked them all soundly
And put them to bed.*
    or,
*She hugged them all soundly
And put them to bed.*

What New Parents Say

Susan, a young mother, looks back on the first few months of her child's life:

> What a hodgepodge! Sometimes we picked her up, sometimes we let her cry. Half the time I didn't know what to do when she fussed. I used to get really mad. I honestly thought that little thing was out to get me.

David, a new father, comments:

> We read that everything you do with a new baby imprints itself forever. We felt we didn't dare make a mistake, so we were very nervous. I'm sure the baby felt it, young as he was. He seemed nervous, too. It took us all about six months to settle down.

Irma says she had to break away from being too rigid with her baby:

> My parents had raised me in the heyday of schedules. I took my cue from them. I can't *believe* some of the things I did. I actually tried to program that baby's bowel movements.

19

New Parent, New Baby

Being a new parent can be a very mixed bag. The new baby is enchanting—small, helpless, precious—but, let's face it, a little intimidating, too. Even if you've done some reading and taken a parenting course. Even if you know how to diaper, feed, and burp. Even if you've had a bassinetful of advice from relatives, friends, your doctor, or the midwife. No matter how strong your support system is, you may find that your baby is truly a little stranger.

Much new parent stress comes from a combination of things. You're tired. You're experiencing a whole raft of changes in your life. And—you somehow have the feeling that whatever you do is going to have an effect on that little character in the bassinet. You're correct to be concerned with the *patterns* of behavior you're setting up in the first months of your baby's life. They *are* important. But with love, common sense, and a few practical suggestions, you can start off on the right foot.

Starting off on the Right Foot

Begin by trusting yourself. You're human. So's baby. Some things will come naturally. But you'll also have to watch your baby for cues. The kind of baby you have will determine in some measure how you act with her. What kind of infant is she? Quiet? Average? Active? Your discipline will have to work within the boundaries of your baby's style.

Resign yourself to the fact that you're going to make some mistakes. But babies are less fragile than you think. No baby's psyche is going to be permanently damaged by having one or two signals read incorrectly. So you thought it was just fussing and it was a genuine gas pain. So you thought it was hunger and it was teething. Forget it. Baby will.

Get certain decisions squared away even before the baby is born, if you can. Some baby-care strategies will come out of necessity. For instance: Is one of you going to stay home with baby for a while or are both of you going to be working? Are you going to share the care? Will you have a house-keeper or relative taking care of the baby on a steady basis?

Or will your child be placed in family day care or in a day-care center? Discuss these things with your spouse.

It might even be a good idea for you and your partner to play "What if?" What if the baby has trouble falling asleep? What if he sucks his thumb? What if he's a poor eater or cries a lot or is afraid of loud noises or strangers? How will you handle it?

Whoever is going to take care of the baby should share your baby-care philosophy. If your parents cuddle your baby but the family caretaker lets her cry, your baby is in for some rough times. All children, even the youngest ones, react badly to "mixed messages."

Mainly, you'll want to give your newborn support and plenty of loving. But this doesn't mean that you have to be slave parents. You can be sensitive to your baby's need to be held and still not drop everything at the first peep from the crib. You can be soothing and attentive during feeding and when your newborn fusses, but you don't have to handle and jiggle her all day long.

The best way to get off on the right foot is to be loving but casual. Keep in mind that a baby is another member of the household, not the only member.

Spoiling

Dance, little baby,
Dance up high:
Never mind, baby,
Mother is by;
Crow and caper,
Caper and crow.

Can you spoil a baby? Not by giving TLC—tender loving care. One psychologist went so far as to say that the disturbances of early childhood usually arise from too little warm attention rather than too much.

Babies are new to the world. They haven't seen much. So their impressions of what life is like come almost entirely from the way you treat them. The warmth, food, cuddling, touching, and soothing, the patterns of sleep and cleanliness that parents and caretakers provide, help shape their basic framework of experience. We know now that a baby's envi-ronment in the first year has a profound effect on later life.

It's useless to be strict with a baby. He's too young to understand it. Obviously, he can't understand punishment either. Although a colicky infant can tax your patience, it goes without saying that you never hit. You shouldn't scream or yell either. Tiny nervous systems don't handle it well. The discipline of infancy consists mainly in setting up patterns that reflect caring, gentleness, security, and, as the baby gets older, a comforting set of routines.

Crying

> Baby, baby, naughty baby,
> Hush, you squalling thing, I say . . .

If there's one aspect of baby behavior we'd all like to discipline, it's crying. There's not a parent alive who hasn't moaned, "If only that baby would be quiet!" A wailing infant is both guilt-producing and anger-making. There's no mom or dad who hasn't rocked that cradle with a little more force than necessary. Sometimes, operating under the strain of no sleep and frayed nerves, or what is sometimes called "baby blues," a parent will actually hit an infant. The parent suffers terrible pangs of remorse afterward. Babies are fragile and the chances of hurting an infant seriously are very real. Watch yourself for symptoms of reaching the end of your rope. Call a relative. Ask a friend to spell you. Don't wait until you're sorry.

As a parent, you have to resign yourself to the fact that crying comes with the territory. There isn't a baby who doesn't cry. Don't look enviously at that quiet infant in the next carriage in the park. If you were to inquire, you'd discover that he cries, too. If he doesn't, there's something wrong with him.

On balance, crying makes all kinds of sense for the survival of children. How else can they let parents know that they're hungry or wet or teething?

There's no way it makes sense to discipline or punish a baby for crying. Nor should you ignore it. But there are ways you can get across the notion that she doesn't have to cry in order to have her needs met.

Infants cry for a number of reasons—hunger, discomfort, inability to release into sleep, even boredom. Some parents think that if they pick up the baby when she cries, it will encourage her to cry for attention. Actually, the reverse is probably true. Letting an infant cry will only make her frustrated and angry, and may make you the same.

It's far better to feed, comfort, and cuddle a crying baby. Your baby may not understand words yet, but he certainly understands that in doing these things for him, you're saying, "I'm here. I'll take care of you. I love you." Susan Crochenberg, associate professor of human development at the University of California at Davis, says, "The more responsive a mother is to her baby, the less it cries, the more securely attached it gets to be and the more readily it develops trust." And Dr. Lee Salk of New York Hospital–Cornell Medical Center says, "Children whose cries are answered learn to vocalize well and not to whine or whimper because they've already found out that verbal behavior is rewarded."

Another reason to respond to baby cries is this: Educators now believe that a certain amount of stimulation is very good for even very young children. So think of it this way. Every time you pick up your crying youngster and hold, burp, pat, and cuddle him or take him on a stroll around the apartment on your shoulder, you're providing an educational experience!

Constant Crying

What about the baby who cries constantly? If you've done everything you can to make your baby comfortable, and she still cries more than a total of two hours a day (that's a long time), you'd better talk the situation over with your pediatrician. Maybe your baby is allergic to her formula. Maybe she has colic, a common infant complaint which usually disappears after about three months. Maybe you're super nervous and the baby is picking up your vibrations.

If the doctor finds that you have a perfectly healthy baby with a higher than average cry factor, here are a few next steps:

- Try to relax.
- Ask a friend or relative to give you a hand.
- Get some hired help if you can afford it.
- Ask your spouse to share the "squall times" with you so that you can get a little more sleep.
- *Don't* decide that you have a "problem" baby.

As Baby Gets Older

As the baby gets older, she will undoubtedly cry less. But the crying will be more sophisticated. She may cry if there are new people around, or if she hears a sudden loud noise, or if she sees you or another caretaker whom she's used to leaving the room.

- She may cry for attention.
- She may cry from frustration.
- She may cry because she's overtired, or hungry, or bored.

Sometimes a word or pat will turn the tears to smiles. Sometimes offering a toy will do the trick. And sometimes just watching what's going on will satisfy. Babies love to be around adults. Why put your offspring in solitary when you can set her up in an infant seat or play pen where the action is?

There's no reason to feel that if your baby wants attention and company from time to time that you'll be spoiling her if you give it. Look at it this way: Your child is beginning to want to take a more active place in the family. She wants to participate. That's a good sign. It means that your early parenting has worked.

Good discipline at this point will be to strike a balance between giving baby play and attention and letting her learn how to be contented on her own.

Sleep

Wee Willie Winkie runs through the town,
Upstairs and downstairs in his nightgown;
Rapping at the window,
Crying through the lock:
"Are the children all in bed?
For now it's eight o'clock."

In the sleep department, babies vary. Some storybook newborns sleep sixteen to eighteen hours a day. Some sleep through the night after a few weeks but are fussy most of the day. Others reverse the process. This last can be the toughest, especially for parents who have to get up and go to work in the morning.

It helps to know that the most bizarre sleeping patterns are usually only temporary. Most babies tend to settle down into a routine of napping once during the day and sleeping through the night by the time they're six months old.

Six months, of course, can seem like a long time if you have a nonsleeper. *Why me?* you may ask yourself. *How come I get the baby insomniac? And does she have to cry just because she's awake?*

Truth is, very young children do not have a whole lot to busy themselves with if they're awake. Once they've eaten and filled a diaper or two, they've been through their whole repertoire, in a manner of speaking. If they're not tired, there's only one thing left. Crying. But give these squallers a few months and they'll be happily kicking their legs, grabbing for the cradle gym, or cooing to their rattles.

Can you train a baby's sleep habits? You can't change an infant's basic sleep chemistry. Wide-awake youngsters are probably going to stay that way. Eventually, they settle into rhythms of sleep that are right for them and don't impinge on you. In the meantime, you can establish some patterns that may make life a little easier. You can certainly get across the idea that there's a time for sleep, even with a young baby.

The first thing to do when your infant won't go to sleep at slumber hours is to check whether anything physical is bothering him. Is he hungry? Does he have a dirty diaper? Cramps? That rare open safety pin? Think about whether a little overstimulation may not be responsible. If your baby has had a roomful of relatives chucking her under the chin, you can't expect her to calm down and pop off on cue. She'll need a little time to wind down.

But if there's no cause for wakefulness that you can figure out, try to encourage sleepy time.

Sleep Inducers

Holding and rocking are time-honored sleep inducers. One mother does a gentle back rub that she claims works. Another couple walk their baby around the apartment in papoose slings. "We take turns wearing her, and the gentle jogging motions sends her off," they say. Some parents say they take their baby out after supper in their carriage. The air and the motion seem to be the things that put certain babies to sleep.

Other parents find that giving the baby a bath after supper guarantees them a quiet period afterward. A record player, music box—almost anything that soothes—is fine, if it works. Here's where being sensitive to both your needs and your baby's comes in.

But sometimes nothing works. In this case, you may have to resign yourselves to being up nights for a few months. Take turns doing the night watch. It can even be fun if you can catch up on your sleep during the days. But if the no-sleeping lasts longer than that, you can't turn your home upside down and pull out a million bags of tricks to get your baby to sleep.

You'll *have* to start easing your baby into the family's sleeping pattern. Put him down at a regular time. You may even have to let him fuss off to sleep on his own for a few nights. Play it by ear; leaving a child screaming for hours doesn't teach him anything. But waiting a few minutes to see if the decibel rate goes down is good infant discipline.

There are a few bright-eyed types who have difficulty releasing into sleep well past the six-month mark. If you have such a one, you should check with your doctor to make sure that there's nothing physically wrong that's keeping him awake. But don't ask for medication to send him to dreamland. Save the drugs for the times when he's truly sick.

If your baby gets into a routine of going to bed at a certain hour every night, she will most likely eventually adjust to being both awake and alone. She'll probably find her own way of drifting off. Blanket-clutching, head-banging, thumb-sucking, and rocking are all ways that clever babies find to put themselves to sleep. Let her work it out for herself. You may want to offer a nighttime breast or bottle feeding. If that works with your baby, fine. Some doctors say use a pacifier, others feel that it puts baby's sucking too much under outside control. You decide.

Get to know how to read your child's signals. Even a very young baby will yawn and rub his eyes when he's sleepy. Learn to seize those moments. Get the baby into the crib and get some sleep yourself.

When you put your infant to sleep, always do it as if you expect him to stay there. But recognize that no amount of

patterning or patting is going to turn bright eyes into a
placid dozer. This doesn't mean that your child shouldn't get
a good idea of when people are supposed to sleep and to be
awake. If your Curious George wants to watch the sun rise,
he should learn to do it quietly, on his own time and in his
own bed. It's a good pattern to establish as early as possible.

Feeding and Eating

Handy Pandy Jack-a-dandy
Loves plumcake and sugar candy.

The Meaning of Food

Food can have many meanings. It's not only something
you eat to stay alive. It can also be social security or reward—
or a means of satisfying cravings far beyond the pangs of
hunger. In the extreme, food can even be a form of punishment. "Then no dessert for you, young lady," says the irate
parent of a non-eating eight-year-old. Early on, babies pick
up these nuances of food meaning. Even the newest newborn
senses that the breast or bottle is a conduit not only to survival
but to satisfaction and security.

No Force, No Fuss

Parents are often unsure that baby is getting enough of
the right kind of food at the right time. Coupled with this
uncertainty are other worries: "I'm not being strict enough
about feeding." Or just the reverse, "I'm probably too rigid
about feeding but I'm afraid that otherwise the baby won't
get enough to eat."

Newborn babies know enough to eat. But not all of them
are interested in food to the same degree. Your baby may be
a lusty eater. On the other hand, she may doze off soon after
she begins feeding, especially in the early weeks. If you're
nursing, you can't see how much nourishment she's taken,
and you may get concerned. You should know that babies
usually get most of the breast milk in the first few minutes.

If you're not nursing and your baby quits on a bottle after
a few ounces, you can *see* how much is left, and that may
worry you. But you can usually be sure she's had enough.
Maybe she can only hold a few ounces at a time.

Should you urge your baby to drink more or nurse longer?

Definitely not. Urging doesn't make an infant nurse longer or drink more. What it will surely do is make him cranky. And he may get the feeling that he's got to stand up for his rights and resist you. Very soon, feeding time will become not a pleasant and relaxed interlude but a battle of wills. You'd be surprised how well even a ten-pound infant can handle this kind of confrontation. Talk about passive resistance!

Remember that no healthy baby ever starved to death. With increasing maturity may come increased capacity. And at a certain time, often at around nine months, appetite may slow down. Not to worry. Don't force. Of course, if your baby doesn't eat for an extended period of time, you'll have to check with the doctor to make sure that there's no health reason for her lack of appetite.

Your baby wants to eat every two hours. Is that too much? Not for *your* baby. Some infants don't follow that neat, every-four-hours pattern. They need more food when they're small and will taper off in their demands later. Babies don't over-eat. So if you have a chowhound, be happy. Feed him. Don't make him bellow for his breakfast! If you do, he may get the idea that he will be fed only if he makes a big fuss. And that's certainly not what you want to tell him. An important part of good baby patterning is *not* to make an issue of food.

How to Feed

Says one father, "I notice that the baby is much more receptive to her bottle when I hold and cuddle her than when I prop the bottle."

And a mother comments, "If I've had a hard day at the office and I've dragged home some of that tension, it's better for me not to feed the baby. He seems to sense it, and gets fussy."

How you feed the baby is part of *parental* discipline. Holding, cuddling, and allowing time for the baby to satisfy her sucking urge gives her a sense that eating is a relaxed time. Loud noises and arguing don't go with eating either. You would avoid a noisy restaurant. Your baby likes to eat in quiet surroundings, too. Keep the loud talk and argument away from baby's mealtime.

Taking Cues from Baby

Eating, like sleeping, is at first a matter of taking your cues from the baby. But as he gets older and his digestion settles down, he can begin to take some of his cues from you.

You can expect that your baby will be on a more or less three-meals-a-day routine within six months. *When* the three meals take place should be scheduled according to your needs as well as baby's. It's good to give the baby the idea that eating is an established ritual, not a sometime happening. If as a couple you were used to pickup meals, you may have to rethink your eating habits. Better decide now whether dinner is going to continue to be casual. Do you want to raise your child to grab a bite whenever? Or do you want to look forward to sitting down at the table together as a family?

Again, if you are both early risers, you can ease baby into a schedule of eating her first meal on the early side. If you're night people, she can often be slowly and gently eased into a later breakfast. There's nothing wrong with a little adjusting on both sides to arrive at mealtimes that work for all of you. Just so long as your baby always gets the message: "See. You can depend on our having food for you every day at about this time. No need to fuss or cry."

You'll notice as the baby gets older that he is willing to wait a bit longer for meals. He's no longer as ferociously hungry as he may have been as a newborn. This is the time to do a little patterning in flexibility. Try coming in from the park a little later, if it's more convenient. Or experiment with pushing supper up a half hour if you're going out for the evening.

This doesn't mean that you shouldn't adhere to a general schedule. And it also doesn't mean that you can't still take some cues from baby. If five o'clock is *always* your baby's low point of tolerance, you should try not to be out walking in the park or on the freeway when the clock strikes five. Just figure that at five o'clock supper should be on the table, for your sake as well as his!

What's to Eat?

What baby eats is as important as *when*. Breast milk is about the best food you can offer your child. But if nursing isn't for you, for whatever reason, there are fine formulas on the market. Your doctor can tell you which one is best for your baby.

A word about solid foods: You'll want to introduce them to the baby slowly, one at a time. Cereal is a good first solid food, because it has iron, which milk does not have.

Parent Food Discipline

Some parents pale at giving baby that gummy-looking stuff that is baby cereal. "How can I warp the poor kid's palate that way?" one parent wailed.

Wait a minute. That's your hang-up, not baby's. And this is the time you will have to be disciplined enough to keep the grimace off your face as you watch your infant spoon up her mush. Cereals and other whole grains are important foods for your baby to get used to. The kid who eats mush at six months will eat his oatmeal at six years, and be the better nourished for it.

If you want your child to be a "good eater" with a healthy attitude toward food, it's a smart idea to introduce a *variety* of foods to him while he's a baby. Introduce them one at a time and slowly. You'll usually get instant acceptance, especially with foods like mashed banana and puréed apricot, because they're sweet. For the same reason, carrots are more likely to produce a grin then green beans. A sweet tooth seems to be standard equipment even for humans who don't have teeth yet!

But just because Little One prefers sweets is no reason to load him up with them. Stay away from cookies, candy, sugar syrups for babies. The natural sugar in fruit is fine, but don't overdo it. You don't want to give your baby the idea that food and sweets are one and the same. What you really want to get across is that in food, *variety* is the spice of life.

How much will your eating habits affect your baby's? A lot. If eating is a pleasure for you, it probably will be for your baby. If you're relaxed about her eating, she'll be relaxed about it. This means tolerating bowel movements while you're nursing her. And, later, it means putting up with some messes as she makes her first attempts to feed herself. Sloppy is the name of the game and if you can be cheerful as you wipe the spinach off the walls, you'll be guaranteed healthy attitudes toward eating.

If you're willing to try new foods, she'll grow up being adventurous about menus. As in every other aspect of disci-

pline, how *you* are will be a model for your child. And it's
never too early to set a good example.

Baby Bowel and Bladder

*A housekeeper puts the baby on the potty at seven months
and reports results.*

*A mother uses suppositories to train the baby to have regu-
lar bowel movements and the baby performs.*

*A father exercises his infant's legs after each feeding, waits
for the inevitable results, and then changes the baby, insisting that he's getting him on a toileting schedule.*

None of this has anything to do with the *child's* toilet
training. In each case, it's the *adult* who's being trained to
catch the baby in the act. Bladder and bowel function is not
under parental control. It's under baby's control. Somewhere between the ages of two and three, your child will
illustrate this. At which time you can give her an assist by
providing a potty seat.

Trying to discipline bathroom habits before that age (and
especially in infancy) is useless. Besides, it creates stress for
both you and the baby. It doesn't make toilet training happen
any faster and may, in fact, slow it down. If you concentrate
too much on this area of your child's life, or act disgusted,
unhappy, or disapproving of natural bodily functions, you
can create big problems. A simple act like diapering, for
instance, can deliver many kinds of messages about elimination, *which can affect later toilet training.*

> Mr. A. diapers the baby clumsily, but he smiles and
> talks to the baby while he does it. "Hey, I'll bet you
> feel better now," he says reassuringly.

> Ms. B. looks at the full diaper, wails, "Oh, no, not
> again." Hastily, she cleans up, her face a mask of
> disgust.

> Mr. C. is furious when he finds his ten-month-old
> playing with his feces in the crib. He yanks the baby
> out of the crib, saying, "Naughty boy."

In each of these cases, the baby probably didn't understand the words. But the tone is unmistakable. It's good
parent discipline to refrain from harsh looks and words over

your baby doing what comes naturally. Constipation and rectal bleeding are only two of the results that can occur if you give baby the wrong message about his messes.

Maybe the idea of "too early toilet training" as a reason for psychological problems has been overstated by Freudian psychologists. Nevertheless, there's plenty of evidence to suggest that pushing the potty chair too early is a very poor idea.

Thumb-Sucking

More than 80 percent of all babies suck their thumbs and/or fingers at least once in a while. Why? To satisfy a strong instinctive sucking urge that they're born with. Most kids outgrow the habit by the time they're a year old. A few hang on until three or four, and a few persist until six or seven. In spite of the fact that most dentists say there's very little chance that early finger-sucking will affect a child's teeth, many parents find it annoying and even embarrassing.

"Thumb out of the mouth," daddy whispers, and gently removes the offending digit. Of course, baby doesn't understand a word of what daddy is saying and will probably pop her thumb back in her mouth as soon as daddy goes away.

Trying to curb the thumb-sucking of infants usually doesn't work. A better approach is to give baby more time at the breast or smaller holes in the nipples on her bottle. That way she'll get more sucking time and be less apt to make up for it with her finger.

Security Objects

Around the age of six months to a year, babies often latch onto a blanket, stuffed toy, or diaper and want to have it with them all the time, particularly when they're sleepy or in a situation where they're feeling strange. Some parents, worried that the baby will become too dependent on it, or that the thing itself will get too disreputable, try to part object and baby.

Not to worry. The "thing" usually falls apart just about the time the child is ready to give it up. One parent watched a child's much-loved blanket disintegrate into tatters and then tear into smaller and smaller pieces. Finally, the child was carrying around a corner of fabric about as big as a coaster. Both parents were worried that if they took the tiny rag away, there'd be a row. But one day the child announced, "All gone," and threw the piece of blanket into the garbage can.

There's no health, discipline, or other reason to separate a child from his "ducky," "lovey," "blankey," or "didee." If it's getting so dirty that you can't stand it, give it a wash and return it to its owner. Letting a baby give up his security object in his own good time is one of the ways in which a child learns self-discipline.

Hand to Mouth

Little Jack Horner sat in a corner
Eating a Christmas pie.
He stuck in his thumb and pulled out a plum
And said, "What a good boy am I!"

How do you find out how a thing feels, whether it tastes good, if it's smooth or rough? Well, if you're a baby, you put it in your mouth. Hand to mouth is the scientific method of babyhood. And a baby's laboratory is the world.

You certainly want to encourage learning. At the same time, a parent is entitled to a cringe or two when Jack pops a cigarette butt into his mouth. Unfortunately, Jack doesn't know a butt from a piece of Danish pastry. So you'll have to save him from himself without telling him that hand-to-mouth experiments are bad.

The easiest way is to simply say, "Thank you," hold out your hand, and take the object if you see it on its way to the mouth. (You may have to be fast.)

Another thing you can do is to say, "Yuck!" with appropriate facial expression. He'll get the idea, especially if you do it several times.

If Jack is old enough to know some words, you can say, "We don't eat cigarette butts. We eat food," and take the object away.

But better than that is an ounce of prevention. Keep yuckies and dangerous nonedibles out of baby's reach. As soon as your infant is sitting up is a good time to start. Expect your baby to put things in his mouth. Give him safe toys to perform his infant experiments on.

Hand to Mouth to Floor

What do you do when Joan plays fetch and you're the retriever? Yes, Joan is deliberately throwing that toy out so that you'll pick it up. This is another way that babies learn. She is testing out the very important principle of constancy. Can I lose this? and get it back? When it comes back, is it the same? So in it goes to the mouth again.

Don't worry about germs, unless your floor is very dirty. Babies can tolerate a few germs. It's more important that your infant try this until you're tired of the game. Of course, you don't have to pick up all afternoon. Luckily, baby Joan is pretty easily distracted.

Independence and Dependence for Infants

So you did it. You gave your infant all that wonderful loving and cuddling. You made sure he got to know his main caretakers. Plus, he relates to them. Does he relate! When you or dad walk into the nursery, he quivers all over. Those giggles, coos, and smiles are mainly reserved for you or others in his family, which may include a sitter or housekeeper.

For a while this tiny dispenser of favors will even dole out smiles to a stranger. But somewhere around six months of age, he may become suspicious of all but his nuclear family. How come? Where did you go wrong? "Spoiled," sniffs grandma as grandson Stevie turns red with rage when she picks him up. "Nervous child," is the family's verdict when little Jane screams her way through the Thanksgiving gathering.

Should you worry if your baby suddenly begins to react badly to new people? No. It's all part of the great growing-up process. Actually, it's a good sign. She's beginning to make choices. It's also a confirmation that you've successfully forged that all-important bond of love. She *prefers* you and the one or two other people whom she's used to. She's letting you know that. That's why her face lights up when you come into a room and why she may cry when you leave it. But how far do you encourage this flattering dependence?

Take this scenario, which may occur anywhere from six months to the end of baby's first year: You get an invitation to a party. But for some time now, the baby has been howling bloody murder if you leave before he's asleep. What do you do? Do you:

- Refuse the invitation, decide not to make any dates for a while, and feel like you're being controlled from the crib?
- Hire a sitter, give her the instructions, and flee, hardening your heart and your eardrums? After all, he has to learn sometime.
- Wait until the baby's asleep, then sneak off and leave him with a strange sitter, hoping he won't wake up?
- Try first to get the *same* sitter or caretaker who usually stays with the baby? Failing that, make sure the baby spends some time with a new sitter before you leave? (An hour's worth of sitter time isn't too much to pay for your peace of mind and the child's.)

The last solution seems to fit in best with sound discipline. You're answering your own needs, that is, having a social life. On the other hand, you're making sure that your baby feels secure in the care of a competent surrogate. You're being responsible but not overindulgent. Above all, you're not gambling with your baby's feelings. You're thinking about how you would feel if *you* woke up to find a stranger bending over you!

One of the goals of discipline is to make a child independent. You showed your infant that he could depend on you. Now you're showing him that you must go away from time to time but that you'll always come back.

A New Season

To everything there is a season, says the old adage. And nowhere is it more true than in raising children.

Somewhere between infancy and toddlerhood, you begin to see evidence that the baby is beginning to be someone with skills—a real person.

He grasps a pacifier, turns himself over, pulls your hair, sits up, reaches for a rattle, shakes it back and forth, makes deliberate sounds, pulls himself up on the crib bars, calls mama, crawls, and wipes mashed potato on the walls.

Baby at one year plus may do all of the above. She has become both investigator and slob. This is the time when you want to encourage independence while childproofing the apartment. It's a time to protect life and property (yours and hers), as well as the crockery. So give the lurchin' urchin room to move and a minimum of sharp corners to fall against. If she falls, let her get up on her own unless you think she's hurt. While feeding, let her try her hand at spooning up the goo. Just cover yourself and the area so the mess is minimal. Babies are neither graceful nor neat when they're first doing things on their own. That's why they need a lot of practice. Give it to them. If you put the brakes on this trial and error or offer too much assistance, baby may slow down on trying anything new.

The same thing goes for language. As your baby starts to talk, help him. Try to get him to use the newly acquired word when he asks for something, instead of grunting as he did before. Reinforce the word. "You want your *duck,* Roger?" It's thrilling when your baby first begins to talk. Keep in mind that it's pretty exciting for him, too. It's a giant step in development to be able to use languge. How much more independent a human can be when he can say what he wants or how he feels. Independence is only one of the areas in which you'll see change as your child leaves babyhood and becomes a toddler.

Chapter 3

Toddler Tactics

Little ships must keep to shore;
Now larger ships may venture more.

What's a toddler made of? This walker-talker-runner-comedian-angel-monster is more spice than sugar, that's for certain. Just when you think he's easy to get along with, he gets difficult. Just when you think she's through with temper tantrums, she throws a corker.

No wonder a parent gets puzzled. You've just gotten a handle on what *babies* are like, and they become toddlers. New people—dynamos of energy who change moods every five minutes and slide into new patterns of behavior every five weeks. What are they doing? Why are they doing it? And what can you do about it?

Every parent of a toddler has experienced some of the pressure points of the eighteen-month to three-year age group. They're a favorite topic on park benches, in stores, living rooms, backyards, and offices. Mothers, fathers, grandparents, and housekeeper-caretakers have mulled them for generations. Believe it or not, the newer model of toddler isn't much different from the old. But let's take a look at the pressure points, one at a time.

Temper Tantrums

Does your kid throw temper tantrums? Adam does. His face gets as red as a beet and you can hear him a block away. I die of embarrassment when he starts up like that.

What's with Adam, the small citizen who throws himself on the floor in the cookie aisle of the supermarket? Is he going bananas at the ripe old age of two? And how are his parents going to keep from going with him?

Adam's temper tantrums certainly seem bizarre. But they're also fairly common. If Adam behaves this way at seven or eight, it's a problem. But at two or three his behavior is quite normal.

It stems from the fact that his controls are still pretty wobbly. His *me* factor is very strong; that is, he's aware of the world pretty much in terms of himself. He concentrates on what *he wants*—to run, to feed himself, to say a word, to get his mother's attention. The problem is, he can't do all of the things he wants to do. And he can't have everything he wants as instantly as he wants it. Sometimes he can't even make up his mind what it is he does want most. For instance, he may be tired and want to go to sleep. But he may also want to stay with his fascinating family in the living room. He can't decide. Pretty soon, those two weighty choices are too much for him. He goes to pieces, and it takes the form of a temper tantrum.

Because temper tantrums are normal, does that mean you as a parent have to let it happen? Absolutely not. This kid needs help. He needs you to save him from himself.

Step-by-Step Rescue

Supposing you have an "Adam" who carries on in the supermarket. The first thing you can try to do is *anticipate*. Maybe you notice Adam is more malleable in the morning. Why not try to schedule your shopping for those hours? And maybe you can plan ahead to keep him busy as you shop. Maybe he can "help." Or maybe there's a little game you two can play. "Let's watch for yellow things. Let me know when you see something yellow. Where are the crackers? Do you see crackers, Adam?" Here you're trying to *distract* (and tossing in some fun learning at the same time).

But what if both anticipation and distraction fail you? What if Adam suddenly goes off like a siren and sweet reason goes out the electric door?

Don't yell or spank. That will just show him that you have as little control as he has.

Don't bribe him with a bought toy or treat. If you do that, you're just rewarding him for making a nuisance of himself and he'll do it again and again.

Deal with it *now*. You'll have to carry him off if he carries on! And do it firmly, simply, and without a lot of discussion. "All right, Adam, we're going to leave the store now." Or, "You can't act this way here so we'll have to leave."

Sometimes this move is decidedly inconvenient. It might help to have the other parent along so that one of you can check out the groceries. The important thing is to keep your cool, as you show that you simply won't allow this behavior.

Down-Home Temper

> Punch and Judy fought for a pie;
> Punch gave Judy a knock in the eye.
> Says Punch to Judy, "Will you have any more?"
> Says Judy to Punch, "My eye is sore."

Temper tantrums aren't confined to the supermarket, as we all know. When they happen at home, you don't have the pressure of strange eyes on you, so in a sense it's easier to deal with.

Sometimes it helps to isolate the child for a while.

"Trisha, that screaming hurts my ears. You'll have to stay in your room until you stop that. When you think you're ready, you may come out." (Make sure *she* controls the coming-out time.)

Remember, you're not in this to break a spirit, just to tame it. Use the isolation technique sparingly, and only when all else fails. *Never* lock a kid in a room, or threaten darkness.

Always try first to find out the "why" behind the outburst. And when you see that you're getting somewhere in the temper-tantrum battle, reward Trisha or Adam. A kiss, a hug, a whispered word or two. "I'm glad to see you're feeling happier." "How grown-up you were in the store today." Or, "I know it was hard for you to wait so long at the doctor's office." Toddlers like to know that their efforts to control themselves are appreciated. Doesn't everybody?

The Why of Tantrums

Sometimes tantrums come on a toddler for no reason at all. Or at least for no reason that you may be able to figure out. But it may cheer you to know that many of them are related to growing—your youngster may be trying to do something, or to learn something, and finding it very frustrating.

It may be something as simple as learning a new skill. Take Petra. Petra tried valiantly to feed herself, but she just couldn't get her fingers working fast enough when she was both hungry and tired. At lunchtime, she came apart.

Shrieking with rage, she threw the carefully prepared lunch on the floor.

Could Petra's caretaker have headed off the storm? Maybe, if she had sensed the moment when Petra was getting to the end of her rope. Maybe she could have said, "I'll use the spoon now, Petra," and stepped in. But maybe she couldn't anticipate the depth of Petra's frustration. Maybe the "last straw" came all of a sudden. So Petra's caretaker now has no choice but to wipe up the mess and bundle Petra off for her nap, with as cheery a manner as she can muster. "That's all," she says, indicating that there are no second chances when you fling your food. (This is not punishment, it's a statement of fact.) "You are tired, Petra. You need a nap," still in the same cheerful but firm tone. (Stating another fact, not using bed as a punishment.)

The carrying-on may end when Petra is put to bed. Or it may not. But at this point Petra should be left alone. Her caretaker knows she's tired and unstrung, so she absents herself. And she doesn't feel guilty about it, either. On the other hand, she's careful not to plop Petra into the crib as though she can't stand the sight of her. She gives her a blanket and a toy, makes sure she's dry and comfortable, kisses her and means it, and makes her exit.

It's probably a relief to Petra that someone is putting a stop to her out-of-hand behavior. She knows that someone is in charge. She's getting the message that her caretaker knows that she was out of control, and is helping her. She doesn't feel disliked for her lack of control.

Working Mothers, Single Parents, and Temper Tantrums

Mothers who work and don't see their kids all day tend to have built-in guilt complexes. The same guilts plague divorced or separated parents. They all sometimes tend to blame themselves for their toddler's temper tantrums.

> "It's because I'm working."
> "She's always worse after she sees her father."
> "As soon as I come home, he goes to pieces."

Most of the evidence suggests that toddler temper tantrums occur if parents work or if they don't, and in two-parent as well as single-parent households. Toddler temper is not the exclusive property of any one group. In some cases, there may be a connection between the family situation and the child's tantrums. Nevertheless, you still have to put limits on the behavior. It's a big mistake to try to make up to a child for other circumstances by allowing him to get into the habit of unrestrained temper displays.

Take Alan and Marcia. Alan is an oil rigger who works in a foreign country. He is away from his family for many months a year. Marcia is reluctant to move with him because she's not sure the job will last. Most of the time the kids don't see much of their father. Marcia feels guilty about that. She also misses Alan's help in the raising of her children. The combination of her guilt and the absence of her husband causes her to give in to her children outrageously. They are allowed much more than small children need. They are bribed out of temper tantrums far too often. It has now gotten to be a pattern that makes being with these children for any length of time a nightmare.

Marcia has to realize that she can't make up to her kids for their father's absence. Nor should she try.

Toddler Fears

Laurie has decided that there is a monster in the closet in her room. She's been doing this a lot lately, coming up with all sorts of fears. Monsters is the latest one. Is this normal for a two-and-a-half-year-old?

Some kids are afraid of monsters. Others fear the dark, or strangers with dark glasses, or even a toy of a certain shape. These fears may seem silly to us, but they're very real to a young child. In a way, they're a good sign. They show that your boy or girl is putting ideas together, even though some of the ideas are clearly too scary to handle.

Helping your child to cope with the normal fear of toddlerhood is a form of discipline. How do you do it?

Dos and Don'ts

Don't dismiss the fear. Don't say, "You don't really think there's a monster in there, do you, Laurie?" Because the fact is, Laurie does think there's a monster there. Better to say, "There is nothing in the closet, Laurie. When you're ready, we'll open up the closet and you will see." Later, you might say, "I'll turn on the light now so you can see that there's nothing in the closet."

Slaying the Monster

At a day-care center recently I heard this conversation:

> No, Michelle, there are no monsters here. No monsters under the sofa. No monsters in the bathroom. No monsters anywhere.

The teacher was reassuring a little girl who said she had seen a monster. She said it calmly and as a fact. Michelle and the other kids (who were listening) were all relieved. They didn't realize that the teacher's firm statement was a kind of discipline.

Situations like this come up all the time at home. It's important to *help* a child conquer fear, and not just let him work it out for himself or make fun of him.

These are concrete ways:

"If you're afraid of the dark, we'll give you a little night light for a while, until you feel safer."

"I'm sorry you had a bad dream. I'll come and sit with you for a few minutes in your room."

On the other hand, you don't have to go overboard accepting a toddler's fears. There's no need to get a child into the habit of staying in your bed. Nor do you have to play the game. Some parents think they should acknowledge the monster and then chase it away. "Yes, yes, I see the monster. Okay, now I'm going to shoo it right out the door. There, it's gone."

This kind of make-believe *may* work for the moment. But in the long run, it's confusing for your youngster, and may delay his understanding of what's real and what isn't. After all, if you say there's a monster there, maybe there really is. And if there is, it could come back when you're not there to take care of it. And so on. So don't enter into a child's monster fantasies. Just accept that he has them, and help him to conquer them.

Body Fear

Sometimes kids at this age develop fears about their bodies. It usually comes from learning that bodies are vulnerable, either through their own experience or through seeing another person. One three-year-old was afraid her arm was going to fall off after she saw an amputee. You certainly can't shield your child from real life, nor do you want to. But understand that sometimes it can be scary to a small person to think: My body can be hurt. I can cut myself. Blood can run out of me. I can break.

It's during this period when you may get the child who overreacts about a skinned knee or a minor cut. Her distress is real, but it may be all out of proportion to the size of her wound. Nevertheless, hold back on that, "It's only a little cut. Don't be a baby." She hasn't learned big from small yet. All she knows is that she's damaged. Be sympathetic. Offer a Band-Aid. If you act supportive, but don't go overboard, you'll be giving her some guidelines for concern about her body. She'll begin to understand that she doesn't have to worry so much about small bumps and bruises. Learning *appropriate* reactions is a valuable form of discipline.

Body fears may show up in other ways. I remember that at about age three, my son Mark suddenly refused to hear the story of *Babar*. "No," he screamed whenever I opened that book. Finally he took it and put it in a toy chest. He refused to open the chest, preferring to lock up whatever dread secret *Babar* had between its pages. He was finally able to tell me about it—he was terrified of the story of the poisoned mushrooms. There, before his very eyes, the elephant had turned green and died from eating the wrong thing.

This was a disturbing idea to Mark, a boy with a splendid imagination. He figured that if it happened to an elephant it could happen to him. And maybe it wasn't only mush-rooms! Who knew what other foods could cause color changes and death? Certainly not a three-year-old boy. At any rate, he didn't want to hear about it. He wanted to get rid of the thing that had scared him. Very sensible, from his point of view.

Of course, he got over it. Most children do get over their fears, whether they be of monsters or mushrooms. Espe-cially if their parents or caretakers don't make too much of them, or too little. Sensible discipline of toddler fears should take into account the struggle youngsters have before they understand what's real and what's imaginary.

Hitting, Biting, Bullying

> Greg is always hitting. He just can't seem to play
> nicely. I don't know where he got that idea. We never
> hit him. I'm really worried he's going to be a bully.

What about Greg, who's always hitting? Is it because he's
a boy, and boys are known for that rough stuff? Surprisingly, there's a germ of truth here, because in our culture
we expect more aggressive behavior from males. Equally
likely is that aggression, like temper tantrums, can be caused
by the toddler's frustration. We appreciate that adults get
frustrated, but we somehow have a harder time understanding children's frustration. What do they have to be frustrated about? we grumble. The world is their Tinker Toy.

You'd be surprised what frustrates toddlers. Big problems, for them. How to say what you want. How to walk
across a playground without falling. How to reach that toy
on the top shelf. But whatever the reason, Greg has to be
taught self-control. How do you do it?

As with temper tantrums, you can try to head it off. When
you see the fight over the dump truck shaping up, you can
remove Greg from the scene, distract him with another truck,
or, if his claims to the dump truck are legitimate, try to
distract the other child. Even if Greg is "right" in the argument, you shouldn't allow him to hit. If he's already done so,
you have to make it clear that it is not the way to handle
problems.

And not with long lectures on sharing. Talking to a two-year-old about sharing is not likely to get results.

If you indicate to Greg by your actions and words that
hitting is not the way to solve things, you better believe it.
If you turn around in the next ten minutes and swat Greg
for something, he'll be confused. He won't know whether to
believe what you say or what you do.

There's no question that children who are hit are more
likely to be long-term hitters themselves. But what if you
never hit and your child does? Then you have to help him
contain his hitting drive. Show him that you won't let him
hit. At the same time, try to get to the root of why he is
wanting to hit (or bite or kick). Give him a chance to tell you
how he feels, if he can. If you can see the reasons for his

behavior, help him to see them. You might say, "Greg, I know you're angry. Jennifer broke your block house. But she didn't mean to do it. It was an accident. Jennifer and I will help you get blocks for a new house."

Tit for Tat?

All well and good. Now what about when Greg is the hittee instead of the hitter? Even parents who don't want their child to be the aggressor want a youngster to "defend himself." So we start complicating things for this little two-year-old. Pretty soon we may say, "It's not nice to hit, but if someone else starts it you should hit back."

This is a pretty big package for a kid to understand. Greg is only two, so the fine points of tit for tat may elude him. When he's older, maybe we can debate passive resistance as opposed to preemptive strikes. For now, a simple "no-hitting" rule will have to do. Even if he gets hit first? Yes. Better not to talk revenge, because it will weaken your case.

Never let Greg hit you, for his sake as well as yours. It's a bad habit and will hurt Greg as much as it hurts you. If no one puts a stop to Greg's expressing his anger this way, he'll begin to feel very guilty about it. And this kind of guilt will do damage.

Another thing that won't work is to try to get him to see the other fellow's point of view. Not yet, he won't. If you say, "Greg, how do you think Jennifer feels when you pull her hair?" you're liable to get a blank stare. Because the truth is, it will be a few more years before Greg can really feel for another human being. It's not that he's cruel, it's just that his sense of other people isn't fully developed yet. He doesn't understand cause and effect enough to know that it's his hair pulling that's making his friend cry. And he's not being mean when he bites; he just doesn't know any better.

A Last Word

Aggressive behavior can be a warning signal at certain ages. A ten-year-old who can't keep her hands to herself has something bugging her. But a toddler who hits or bites or kicks is mainly just acting her age. Experimentation may seem more like aggression than it really is.

No, No, No

It seems like the only word Sara can say is "no." She even says it when she means "yes." I don't understand it; she used to be such a sweet child.

Let's take a look at some of the things a toddler may say "no" to: Hugging and cuddling, going outside, staying inside, eating, getting dressed, getting undressed, playing with another child, picking up toys, sitting on the potty, going to sleep, going to the store, to the doctor, to grandma's, or to have a haircut.

Pretty long list. And you probably have a few hundred items from your own toddler to add to it.

It's important to know why your formerly "easy" child is giving you such a hard time. One of the reasons is because it's independence year. She or he is learning how to make decisions. What to do, what not to do. How to *choose*. But independence is a two-way street. She's trying to break away a little bit at the same time you're giving her limits. (After all, she learned the word "no" from you.)

So you two will have to come to a meeting of the minds. You can't say no to everything. If you do, the force of it will wear away. And you may curb Sara's independence and spunk more than you mean to. On the other hand, she can't have her own way on everything. You'll have to decide what's important.

The Important Nos

You have to say no to things that are dangerous, and implement them with swift action. *No* is for:

> *Dangerous things*—going into the street, playing with electric plugs and cords, touching the stove, refusing to wear a seat belt.
> *Things that hurt*—pulling the cat's tail, hitting people, throwing things at the baby.

Other Techniques

For some toddler behavior, you may find that you can work out techniques other than confrontation. For instance, if your busy three-year-old can't hold still while you zip him up, instead of "If you don't hold still we won't go to the park," you might try a little *distraction*: "Here, hold your teddy bear while I zip you up."

Anticipation is another way to go. If you don't want your wandering two-year-old to crash into the good china, it makes sense to stash it out of reach. Removing the objects before they're broken saves hassle. Occasionally, it may pay to ignore some bit of out-of-bounds behavior if it isn't crucial. At other times, you may get the best results from a pleasantly authoritative statement: "Let's pick up the toys now so we can go to meet daddy."

You'll have to find your own happy medium between under- and overdisciplining. If you find that you're always laying down the law, you'll want to take a look at the discipline picture. If, on the other hand, you get a sense that your toddler's life (and yours) is too chaotic, you might want to establish some firmer boundaries.

All this is not to say that "no" is going to disappear. It is only to tell you that being able to say it is an important part of a person's growing, even though it may be a "growing pain" for you.

There's another point about "no." It's not so terrible if your child is allowed a few. In fact, it may be very good.

"No kiss good night tonight? Okay, sleep tight. See you in the morning."

"Do you want to have a haircut today? No? Okay, we'll go tomorrow."

None of this is in the realm of spoiling. It just tells your toddler that you respect the fact that she has a mind of her own.

Discipline is deciding which things you are going to insist on.

Toilet Training

This is the way we wash our hands,
Wash our hands, wash our hands,
This is the way we wash our hands
So early in the morning.

When?

When should you start it? When your child begins to show an interest in the toilet and what it's for. When she's mastered some of the other bathroom business—brushing teeth, washing up, combing hair. When she can talk about elimination and make some connection between her urges and the result. And when she's old enough to understand that there's a time and a place for certain things.

This last one may be the most difficult. When you look at it from the tot's point of view, it requires a great deal of tolerance for *ambiguity* to understand what the adult world is telling her:

> It's okay to urinate and defecate. In fact, we'll make a big fuss over you if you do it at the right time and in the right place. Otherwise, we'll be unhappy with you. We expect you to control those muscles, but only sometimes.

The other thing that children are often confused about is the product itself. Little tots have very hazy ideas of what is dirty or unsanitary. They view their movement as something that's part of them. That's why a surprised mom may find that Jack or Joan cries when the precious bowel movement is flushed down the toilet.

Toilet training is an important part of discipline. But to do it right, you have to first realize the complexity of the ideas that a child must sort out in order to live comfortably in the world of plumbing.

That's why toilet training has to be in step with a child's development. You can't rush it. On the other hand, you don't want to drag it out past the time that the child is ready. So when you feel your child is interested, seize the moment.

How to Do It

The first thing to do is to set the stage. That means having a potty in the bathroom for a while and letting your youngster get used to it. (*Don't* use it for a toy chest or a storage closet.)

After a few weeks you might begin to encourage him to sit on the potty without clothes at a time when he's likely to have a movement. Or right *after*. Praise him if he manages to do what he's there for, but don't overdo it. And don't make him feel no good if he doesn't do anything.

You'll soon be able to take your cue from your toddler. The important thing is to play it by ear. By letting him play with a minimum of clothes on for a while, he'll be ready to sit on the potty quickly if the spirit moves him. Encourage his going by himself, but don't force it.

Don't take diapers off at naptime or at night until your child has been dry for quite some time. Usually kids get trained during the day much more quickly than at night. And if you remove diapers too soon, they may feel they've failed if they don't stay dry.

Actually, there's no formula for toilet training. The best rule of thumb is to ease the youngster into it, and not make it a punishing experience. Remember that some kids take longer than others. But look at it this way. When your Jack and Joan are age thirty, no one will know whether they were trained at two, two-and-a-half, or three. There's no sense in giving a kid hemorrhoids for the sake of a few months of being dry. It doesn't matter if you use a few more boxes of Pampers. It will happen, all in good time.

Discipline in the Day-Care Center

A good place to pick up hints on toddler discipline is at a well-run day-care center. On a recent morning at Bank Street's Infant Care Center, a whole series of minidramas presented themselves:

Lily, one year old, wanted mommy to stay in the center with her. Her mother had been there for a while but it was time to leave. Lily cried when her mother left, even though her mother assured her that she would be back soon. Meanwhile, Kevin, eighteen months old, saw Lily crying. He remembered his sadness earlier in the day when *his* mother had left. He began to cry, too. The teacher picked Lily up and cuddled her and held her. Another teacher distracted Kevin. Then the teacher took Lily for a little walk around the lobby of the building until she stopped crying. She told Lily that her mom would always come back.

What the teacher did:

The teacher, Amy, understood Lily's feelings of abandonment. She comforted her and took her outside so she wouldn't upset Kevin. She also told Lily a comforting truth, that her mother would always come back.

What she didn't do:

She didn't tell Lily that her mother would be right back (a lie) or tell her to "stop crying and be a big girl," which is beyond Lily's capabilities right now.

Two girls were playing at a long table. One girl had all the playdough. The teacher said, "Lois, you have all the playdough. Will you give some to Sherrill, so she can play?" Lois gave Sherrill a tiny piece of playdough and Sherrill began to play with it.

What the teacher did:

She showed Sherrill that she couldn't just take the playdough away from Lois. She had to *ask* for it. Since Sherrill doesn't talk yet, the teacher did the asking. And she gave Lois a choice. She could decide whether to give Sherrill playdough or not.

What she didn't do:

She didn't force Lois to share. And she didn't make fun of her for giving Sherrill such a small piece.

Alexander was awakened by one of the teachers after a long nap. Alexander was cranky when he woke up and he took his crankiness out on the teacher.

What the teacher did:

She held Alexander and hugged him and said, "Alexander is angry at me because I woke him up."

What she didn't do:

She didn't act cross with him or tell him he was being cranky and unpleasant. She acknowledged Alexander's right to be cranky, while trying to cuddle him out of it.

At snacktime Sam wanted a cracker. He made grunting noises in the general direction of the crackers. The teacher knew that Sam could talk if he wanted to.

What the teacher did:

She said, "You can tell me what you want, Sam." In this way, the teacher showed Sam that he could make his wishes known. He could control his wants.

What she didn't do:

She didn't allow him to indulge in more babyish ways of asking for something.

Before lunch the teacher said, "You two girls who have been playing with playdough will want to wash your hands and maybe go to the potty."

One girl shook her head vehemently. "No."

What the teacher did:

She said, "Oh, Joanne, you don't want to go to the potty? Okay. Just wash your hands."

What she didn't do:
She didn't insist or pressure Joanne to the potty. Still, she got across the idea that the hand-washing was important.

David had built a handsome block construction which he said was his boat. Evan was about to knock it down. The teacher intervened.
What the teacher did:
She said, "David made that, Evan. It's David's boat." And she took the young demolition expert away.
What she didn't do:
She didn't allow Evan to break David's creation. Nor did she allow them to fight it out.

In every case, the teacher was using principles of discipline. She was educating and teaching patterns of behavior. But with such a light and fine touch that you hardly knew it was happening.

Actions Speak Louder Than Words

If there's one key to disciplining toddlers, especially at the "no" stage, it's the rule of action. You don't deal successfully with a two- or even three-year-old through long-winded discussions. Nor do you wait very long between when an act is committed and when you respond to it. Time is of the essence.

For instance, some things that toddlers try to do are downright dangerous. They require a swift response. If your lurchin' urchin is headed for the hot barbecue grill, you don't have time to establish a dialogue. You just grab him and take him out of harm's way.

Even under calmer circumstances, you can't go into a long story about *why* you want your child to stop doing something. Toddler memory is short. So is concentration. Step in and stop the behavior. You can talk later.

The same thing goes for question-and-answer games. If it's bathtime beware of asking your two-and-a-half-year-old if she wants a bath. You're almost sure to get a resounding NO. If you simply say, pleasantly and firmly, "It's bath time now," you eliminate the choices that the little citizen is not equipped to make.

Dr. Leah Levinger suggests that sometimes a "thank you" combined with action can work like magic. The toddler who has grabbed dad's favorite cassette tape will usually turn it over promptly if you hold out your hand and say "thank you." Similarly, the open pin, the dog's bone, and other undesirable playtoys are almost always yielded up more or less gracefully when "thank you" accompanies your outstretched hand.

Actions speak louder than words with toddlers. But a few well-chosen words, coupled with action, may be the optimum combination.

A Last Word on Toddlers

In a general way, toddlerhood is the time to discipline dangerous things—running in the street, hurting oneself. It's the place for boundaries on motor activity and removing dangerous or perishable objects from the toddler.

It's also the time to control dangerous behavior—hitting, biting, temper tantrums—before it gets to be a habit.

Toddlerhood is the stage to help your child establish order in the physical world—a place for things, a time to come and go, concepts of how things "work" in the world.

Toddlerhood is the place for encouraging some independence, too. Encourage your child in the use of language (even if it all comes out "no" for a while). Be confident that he or she will one day soon express feelings instead of crying. Encourage your child to talk about fears and feelings. Be supportive of his efforts to do for himself. If he says, "Me do it," let him try.

Show the toddler that he is loved and his ideas are respected. Love and respect are the most important things that you can model. Begin to give him an idea of what you think is *right*. But make sure these things are within his grasp. For example, a toddler won't understand that he must be polite to a neighbor. But he can know that biting is not allowed. Gradually, he will come to understand that biting hurts people. That's the beginning of building conscience.

Be understanding about a toddler's fears. But don't give him long lectures about why he shouldn't be afraid of the dark, because he won't be able to follow them.

A toddler's self-control, or lack of it, is very much dependent on how much she wants parental approval. If you've established a good bond between you, your little dynamo may stray from the accepted path, but she can always be brought back on track by her desire for your approval.

Now is the time for balance. Too many prohibitions may slow down the growth of independence. But too little discipline is a form of neglect.

Chapter 4
Threes, Fours, Fives

Fishes swim in water clear,
Birds fly up into the air,
Serpents creep along the ground,
Boys and girls run round and round.

Portrait of the Preschooler

There's a world of difference between toddler and pre-schooler. The changes may creep up on you, being with your youngster every day. But they would dazzle you if you spent some time with a group of twos at a day-care center and then watched some threes and fours in a nursery school setting.

The toddlers are as they have been described—all impulse. Touch, scribble, drum, pound, smear! Blow a bubble here, push a truck there. They try everything. But their tries are brief. So are their sentences. And their moods. There are quick shifts—from laughs, to tears, to quiet play, to temper.

But peek in at a group of threes and fours (and certainly fives) and you'll see something new in the scene.

These more mature small citizens will be playing. And playing *together,* in groups of two and three. They'll be concentrating—on blockbuilding, or clay modeling, or complicated doll corner play. Most important, they'll be exchanging ideas.

"Put that block over here—over here! Make the castle taller. Make it as tall as the world."

"We're playing monsters. I'm a monster. Do you want to be a monster?"

"Do you like this celery? I like it. I'm going to ask my mommy to buy celery."

"I'm painting. Should I paint you? (Joking.) I'm going to paint on you."

Other child (with smiling assurance): "No, you're not."

55

The Years of Magic

Most parents breathe a sigh of relief when their children get to be this age. Some *prefer* it to any other age. Said one father, "I love learning about the world through Michael's eyes. I have the sense that now I'm dealing with a thinking person. It's fun to see the wheels turning and to know that my child and I can talk to each other, even though I'm aware that his idea of the *meaning* of the words is sometimes different from mine."

It's also satisfying to see the direct cause-and-effect nature of your words and actions. You watch your preschooler absorb and process ideas and then send them back, sometimes in forms that surprise you with their originality. Indeed, these may be what the late Selma Fraiberg called "the magic years."

What does this rich developmental stew mean in terms of discipline?

It means that at three—if you've been a loving but consistent disciplinarian—you're likely to see some of the fruits of your labor. By three—hallelujah!—your offspring will recognize certain routines—washing up, toileting, eating, cleanup, even going to sleep. She'll be able to play both by herself and with others. She can stay in a room alone for a time and amuse herself. She can remember to do some things without being told.

Developmentally, your three will tend to be a "yes" person. She'll *want* to agree, to conform, to please, almost as much as at two-and-a-half she seemed to take delight in saying "no." She'll be more secure, more stable, more sharing. She'll love new words, and even new situations. This hiatus may not last long, however. Sometime before she gets to four, she may start stuttering or tripping over things or in general acting uncoordinated. If that happens, you'll know that she's on the rocky path toward the plateau of four.

Four will not only be learning to dress herself, she'll also be freely expressing herself.

"I'm hungry as a crocodile."

"I have sand in my bathing suit."

"I love grandma best."

The other side of this colorful conversationalist may be her "out of bounds" tendency. She may break things, run away, get lost, lie, swear. She's apt to be one tough customer at times, but will charm you with her very boisterousness.

By five you may be able to enjoy some calm waters. Calm, friendly, cooperative, five may actually seem to enjoy doing the right thing. With luck, you'll have some smooth sailing here. But not entirely. Five may be overambitious. He may feel so competent that he'll have to be restrained from taking risks. He may resent help when he needs it most. He'll be a mixed bag, the fellow of five.

An Internal Government

Somewhere around four or five, according to Selma Fraiberg, "we see signs of an internal government in the personality of the child." It didn't get there by itself. It is this internal government, in fact, that your discipline has been working toward. It doesn't happen all of a sudden and even now, its progress is uneven. At three, and even at four and five, the preschooler is only a step away from anarchy. Discipline has to keep helping to put his feet on firmer ground.

You can aid this process by using your child's newfound ability to communicate. Ask what's wrong. Give your reasons for wanting a certain behavior. But don't overdo the verbal. Don't go on and on or you'll lose him. And don't make the mistake of abandoning action altogether. Understand that in times of stress, your preschooler's newfound internal government may go out the window. At these times you'll want to avoid weak directives or a tremor in your voice. You'll want to come on strong.

What sort of problems in discipline are likely to come up with a preschooler? How much should you insist on? How much can you let slide?

As always, it's better to work to accentuate the positive side. That is, congratulate the good rather than confront the bad, if you can. Again, this doesn't mean closing your eyes to outright naughtiness. It means working with the plus side of three, four, five. The magic part.

Making Magic

These are the years for making magic. This is the time when children learn what is real through flights of fancy and discover the concrete world through make-believe. Above all, this is the era of the imaginary friend, that gremlin who sits at your dinner table and eats nonexistent eggs and takes the rap for your youngster's misdeeds.

"I didn't turn the record player on. The *homongula* did it."

"The *teddy bear* broke the dish. He's so bad."

How come imaginary friends belong in a discussion of discipline? Because that invisible *glerch* or *snerp* or *gremlin* is all bound up with Tommy's and Jill's and Sarah's budding sense of conscience and sense of right and wrong.

Here's how it works when you're three or four years old:

Say you badly want that model airplane of your brother's that's sitting on the kitchen table. You've been told it's "hands off." And you've left behind the babyish wish gratification of two and a half. No more "I won't" and temper tantrums for you. You enjoy parental approval too much. Still—that airplane looks like great fun. So you get up on a chair and help yourself. When accused of the foul deed you smilingly deny everything. You didn't do that. Your friend *Toad* did it.

What a transparent lie! And yet when you think about it, it's pretty ingenious that so many three-four-fives have arrived at such a clever way to avoid guilt.

Should You Discipline Imaginary Friends?

How do you, as a parent, deal with this? Laugh? Spank? Treat it as a lie? A joke?

Making magic and creating fantasy are *good* for kids. Even an occasional raid on property or pantry by *Ghost* or *Toad* need not be dealt with too harshly. You might say, "Tell *George Ghost* that he'd better keep his invisible hands off other people's things." That helps to deliver the message to the right party without entirely wiping out the face-saving device. And you'll be happy to know that this "stage" of using magic friend as fall guy doesn't usually last too long. However, if you find that your youngster is lingering too long or too often in fantasy land you'll have to call a halt. If you have a child who constantly misbehaves and tries to avoid blame you might take a sensitive look at your total discipline picture. Are there too many rules? Is there too much blaming? Are you expecting more "good" behavior than your youngster is capable of, and has he brought in his imaginary friend to help lay off some of the blame? Maybe your child is a little immature and not yet able to accept the consequences of his own actions. Or he may value your approval so much that he'll do or say anything not to have you angry. You will know better than anyone else whether it's normal make-believe or a warning signal.

Learning and Competence

One, two, button my shoe,
Three, four, shut the door . . .

The bases for a child's learning skills are set up early in life. Competence, attention span, ability to solve problems and to think creatively—these patterns start to develop even before children talk. Certainly they are well along by the time the youngster is a preschooler.

Your child has been picking up large gobs of information since he was born. Learning to feed himself, talking, identifying "the moon in the sky." He's managed to acquire some terrific skills. Now, at three, four, and five, learning is beginning to take on a more visible face. He's becoming *competent* in a number of ways.

What does competence have to do with discipline?

One of the jobs of discipline is to help a preschooler enlarge and direct learning, without putting *pressure* on the child or giving him more than he can handle.

Here's a simple competence guideline:

Directions

See to it that your youngster can handle simple directions, such as how to operate the family seat belts (*always*, not sometimes!). Make sure she understands traffic signals and other safety rules and can follow them in a set order: "First you look both ways. Then you . . ." etc. Whether you're cooking or teaching a kid to dress herself, the following of a one, two, three order of things is a good discipline for learning. Just think of how the world works and how many things are based on following a set of directions.

Health Habits

It's better here to have a few rules and stick to them, rather than insist on fastidiousness beyond a preschooler's abilities. One parent we know laid down too many laws for her four-year-old. He was supposed to remember to come in through the mud room, take off his boots, hang up his mittens, wash his hands, hang up the towel, be careful not to let the dog out, and tuck his shirt in. The mother became a nervous wreck insisting on this list, and the boy was on the way, too. Fortunately, the mother realized that it was too much and eased off, with good results.

Chores

Four- and five-year-olds can learn to be pretty reliable at taking over a *simple* job—setting the table or emptying the wastebaskets or helping to gather up laundry. "But it's easier to do it myself," is the cry of the busy parent. Sure. But what does that say to your child? That mommy or daddy is supposed to do everything? That people do things for children, but children don't have to do anything?

Don't invent *meaningless* tasks. Kids catch on to make-work, even at three or four. But if there's a job worth doing that needs to be done, there's nothing wrong in asking your little one to take it on. A word here about *payola*—it's a bad idea to pay for your youngster's cooperation. The best reward is a sincere "Well done!" from you.

Help your child to remember her responsibility if she should forget. Don't expect that she will remember every time. Especially, don't give your preschooler the sole responsibility for a life-or-death task—like caring for the goldfish. She's not ready for that. (Neither are the goldfish.)

There's a great temptation to abandon the whole system if your youngster forgets or slacks off. This is where discipline comes in, yours as well as hers. If it's within the child's scope, you should insist on these small commitments, gently but firmly. What you're doing is laying the groundwork for remembering those term papers and homework assignments later on.

Attention Span

When your child gets to school you'll begin to hear a lot about it. What? Attention span. In both adults and children, it's the ability to finish a task, or at least to spend some time trying. Some people are better at it than others. Some children develop it later than others. All children benefit from some gentle patterning in this direction.

Here's Betty, age three, for example. She's sitting on the floor at home, working at a simple puzzle. She knits her brows in furious concentration as she tries to fit the pieces in place. The babysitter feels sorry for little Betty. She's dying to help her. But maybe she shouldn't rush in this second. Maybe she should give Betty a chance to figure it out for herself. Playing, after all, is Betty's work. Maybe she should be left to it. Maybe the sitter should at least wait until Betty asks for help.

Norm, on the other hand, may present a different picture. It's hard to get Norm to sit down to a puzzle at all. At best, he'll glance at it for a minute on his way from one running game to another. Norm's motor runs overtime. Is he one of those very physical types who will have trouble settling down to sedentary work for a while? Or is he genuinely lacking in attention span? Sometimes a youngster like Norm is sending up the first flares that signal that he's hyperactive, or that he has a problem that needs looking into. But maybe Norm just needs to have someone say to him, "Let's try this puzzle together once." Or, "Don't give up, Norm. I know you can do it."

It's important at this time to begin to be aware of your child's attention span. Have you got a child who can stick with a toy or game or book for a reasonable length of time? Or have you got a child who rushes from one thing to another helter-skelter with no plan and no direction?

If you have a child who can't "settle down" for even a few minutes, it might be wise to figure out how you can improve attention span. Kids sometimes rush from one thing to another if they have too many things to choose from. Perhaps offering a few toys or one or two books may be the way to discipline a child who seems unable to settle down for even a few minutes.

What you don't want to do is to force. This will only succeed in turning off any interest the child has in the subject, be it a game or a book. It's obvious how wrong this route is by how silly it sounds.

"Now you just sit there until you figure that out."

"Now I want you to play with that for a half hour!"

You really can't punish or threaten a child for not having a longer attention span. What you can do is encourage stick-to-itiveness in positive ways. And set the example yourself. If you're engrossed in your work, you're a model for your youngster. The preschooler who "copies" mom or dad working quietly and steadily at a task is picking up valuable tips on competence. So let your youngster watch and play nearby while you're cooking, writing a letter, doing woodworking, or even changing a light bulb. You'll be surprised at how much he'll learn this way.

Another good way to encourage all forms of competence is through praise. Tying shoes, buttoning buttons, putting a puzzle together, painting a picture—these are all terrific accomplishments for a three-, four-, or five-year-old. Appreciate them. Let your youngster know you do. This will make her want to do more of the same. It is a general rule of thumb that the four- or five-year-old who can settle in to *play* with concentration and absorption is the youngster who is able to later settle down in school.

TV and Books

What about TV? Does it encourage or discourage competence and attention span? Opinions vary. Noted child development expert James Hymes thinks it's a total waste of time for children under six. Our view is that it's okay *in moderation*. If the program involves the child (*Mr. Rogers* or *Captain Kangaroo*, for example), it's better. If it's merely a "babysitter," that's not so good. And certainly unlimited TV will give your child attention span only for TV.

Books, on the other hand, are a real stimulus to the imagination. Encourage your youngster to take care of books and put a few always within reach. Well-illustrated books are one of the nicest ways to hold a kid's attention. And you'll set the stage for the discipline of learning to read if you read *with* your child. Educators agree that children who read well and enjoy books usually pick up the habit from sitting on the lap of someone they love and listening to a familiar and favorite story.

Friends and Enemies

Children at this age need to be with other children. And they get along well with them. Preschoolers will often play together nicely for a considerable period of time. But what do you do when the inevitable conflicts arise? If your preschooler comes out swinging, you may still have to referee, holding the hitter and firmly restating an idea he's heard many times before—that he is not allowed to hurt people.

Sometimes young children have to get rid of their anger

in a physical way. If you think this is the case with your preschooler, you might suggest that he hit something that won't be hurt. In other words, go punch out your teddy bear. Whack the pillow.

More often than not you'll be running into another kind of fighting—spitting and bad-mouthing the adversary. "You're a *doo-doo* . . . you *stinkpot* . . . you *BM*." Believe it or not, this is a step forward. It signals that your offspring has traded his fists for a mouth.

Sometimes you may choose to stay out of such a controversy. Usually, the storm blows over, and the stinkpot is rehabilitated. Some parents don't feel it's necessary to intervene if no blows are exchanged. But many parents are offended by gross language. If it bothers you, you should tell your youngster so in no uncertain terms. It may help to offer the child some acceptable way of expressing anger. One geologist we know suggested his son call a temporary enemy an *igneous rock*. A perfectly harmless scientific term, it had the right ring to the youngster's ear.

Brothers and Sisters

> *Molly my sister and I fell out*
> *And what do you think it was all about?*
> *She loved coffee and I loved tea*
> *And that was the reason we couldn't agree.*

There's a different kind of conflict that comes up between siblings. It isn't confined to this age group, but it's certainly not absent either. It may involve hitting (since people tend to hit the people they know best long after they know better). Even if your preschooler doesn't hit his sister or brother, you're likely to get hit with a barrage of words.

"Why can't I stay up as late as Roger does?"

"Sandy pinched me."

"I wish that ugly baby was dead."

How do you handle this unpleasantness? You can't ignore it. You can't squash it, either. You have to recognize that small wars occur in the best of families. But you don't have to put up with unlimited escalation.

You should keep your older child or children from bullying the younger ones.

You should keep the younger one or ones from trading on their favored position as "babies."

You should indicate that you understand jealousy toward the new baby. Mainly, you'll have to act and say (over and over again) that you value a family that cares about one another. It's important at every age to keep *saying* what your values are. Or else, how will your kids know?

The Social Whirl

At this age, sometimes parents and caretakers get so enthusiastic about how well Joey or Sharon gets along with other children that the child is whipped around from one social engagement to another.

"We'll take Bonnie for lunch today and Cindy can go to your house tomorrow." This is a nice idea once in a while, but watch that you don't overdo it, especially with children who spend part of the day in nursery school.

What if you have no choice in the matter? If work or other obligations necessitate your taking your child to a neighbor or a sitter after school, at least try to fortify him with a nap or rest beforehand, or set up the sitting arrangement so he gets some time to rest after he gets there. Very few pre-schoolers can stand the pace of a whole day of socializing.

If you notice your child getting cranky, or bossy, it may be the result of too full a social life. You may be in for discipline problems if you don't see to it that your youngster has some relaxed time alone. One parent refers to it as "down time"— that is, time when the child doesn't have to be friendly or cooperative or on company behavior. We all need down time once in a while.

New Experiences

There's a funny kind of competition in raising kids. Parents want their children to behave well in public places and they're embarrassed when they don't. It's the same nagging embarrassment that leads to rage in the YMCA, and agony in the doctor's office. Very often it has to do with how well your youngster handles new experiences.

When my children were three, four, and five, I always felt that other kids handled new experiences better than they did. Looking back, I see now that this wasn't so.

Most children this age have trouble with newness/change. Whether it's the swimming lesson, a birthday party, or nursery school, many preschoolers begin by balking. It's the rare three-, four-, five-year-old who settles into a new situation without some problem. Often the brightest youngster sees the greatest number of negative possibilities in something new. But what do you do about it?

Most times it helps to turn the event around and try to figure out what the kid may be feeling.

Haircuts

Let's take the haircut, for example. From a child's viewpoint, it goes like this: You get put in a chair, there's a fellow or gal who comes at you with a machine that makes noise and takes away something that's part of you!

Not pleasant, when you think about it that way. So can you say "you must"? Better maybe to creep up on the business. Let the child go with a parent a few times, to get used to the place and procedure. Or, if it really bothers your son or daughter, give home haircuts for a while.

Doctors and Dentists

Visits to dentists and doctors should be prepared for. Especially if your child has to go to the hospital, advance preparation is tremendously important, if there's time for it. Dragging a kid kicking and screaming into a doctor's or dentist's office or into a hospital is not the way to go, and can leave scars that no MD can fix. But unlike the haircut, you can't avoid this one. Here overreassurance may be as bad as no reassurance. Better to say that the injection is going to hurt, if you're asked. Or tell what the medical procedure will be and make it clear that it's a "must."

Nursery School

Nursery school is another one of those new experiences. It should be fun and wonderful for your child. But it's sometimes hard to remember that's what you meant it to be, when your child acts like you're dragging him off to a concentration camp.

"Why doesn't Max appreciate what we do for him?" wailed one mother.

There are a few golden rules to negotiating a successful nursery school experience for three-, four-, and five-year-olds. These guidelines can be applied, with obvious modifications, to day care, summer playschool, swimming lessons, gymnastics, etc. Here they are:

- Introduce the idea well before it's going to happen. This gives Max time to get used to the notion.

- Scout the scene thoroughly. (If a nursery school won't let you visit, cross it off your list.) Make sure that the teachers are qualified, that the equipment is good, that there's adequate supervision. Spend some time watching the teachers in action. Both parents should go along, if possible. Watch the way the kids are treated—how, for example, teachers handle fights, destructiveness, shyness, pants-wetting, thumb-sucking. Does the teacher make the kids do things in a harsh manner? Does she shame them, ignore problems, insist on strict obedience and induce guilt? Conversely, does the place seem utter chaos, kids wandering around unsupervised? If either of these extremes exists, it's probably not the best place for Max (or any child).

- After you've chosen the school, take Max to visit. (After all, he's the one who's going to go there.) He may like it immediately, in which case you will be home free for a few hours. More likely, he'll still have doubts that he wants to give up his parents' company for all that time. So—you may have to wean him away from you gradually.

- Give Max a chance to adjust by leaving him for short periods at first. *Never* tell him that you'll be right back if you won't.

- *Never* threaten or use the nursery school as punishment: "If you don't stop crying, I'll leave you here."

- *Never* sneak away. Either you or the teacher (or both) will feel the brunt of that. On the other hand, don't hang around longer than necessary. If you feel that the school is good, the time ripe, and Max active and involved, don't be afraid to leave. Often children have a "lag"; that is, they keep up the weeping a little bit after they're really feeling sad.

You can judge this; if the teacher tells you that Max stopped crying before you were around the corner, you're probably right to figure he's adjusted.

One more caution: If something is going on in your house—a new baby, illness, divorce—this may be the time to soft-pedal the new experiences. Don't give young Max too much to handle at one time.

Coming and Going

When I was about four, my father used to take me walking on Sundays. When I wasn't looking, he would suddenly leave my side and hide from me. I would turn around, see that he was gone and be terrified. I can still remember the feeling of utter panic that washed over me. In a moment or two he would pop out of a doorway or driveway, laughing. It was just a game to him, but I never got used to it. I'm sure if he had realized how much it scared me, he would not have done it.

Just how strongly coming and going figure in a preschooler's life can be seen when you listen to a group of children playing "house."

"Don't worry, dolly. Mommy will be right back!" says three-year-old Jeannie. Boisterous four-year-old Nan has a tougher approach.

"You're a bad doll, and I'm going to leave you here *all by yourself*."

Five-year-old Danny tells a story which ends, "The boy ran away and they never, never found him again."

As three-, four-, and five-year-olds make their way into the world, they make their peace with it, one way and another. But it's not always smooth sailing. They worry about events that separate them from their parents and caretakers. It's a bad idea to feed on these fears in disciplining your child. The fear of the loss of parental love, and of being abandoned, is very real to preschoolers.

Never, never threaten a child with abandonment. Don't say, "If you don't stop that I'm going to leave you here alone." Or, "If you don't behave I'm going to go away."

A child's threat to leave may be the other side of this abandonment coin. He may use the thing he fears the most to threaten his parents with.

"I'm going to run away," says the angry four- or five-year-old.

And his parent feels pain when, actually, it's a kind of compliment. It means that the worst form of punishment in the child's repertoire is to threaten that the family be separated.

Mothers and fathers sometimes allow their hurt feelings to push them into mean responses:

"Good. I'll even help you pack."

Or

"Don't forget your toothbrush."

Or

"Fine. And don't come back."

None of these approaches seems to put the finger on the problem. For one thing, all of them are hurtful to the child. And none of them teach the child anything. What should you do when your preschooler says that he or she is going to run away? For starters, you could ask:

"What is making you so angry, Jeff?"

"Let's talk about what's bothering you, Amanda. Maybe you'll change your mind."

Maybe Jeff or Amanda needs reassurance.

"I won't let you run away. I love you and need you."

"Maybe you need some time to yourself. How about running away to the backyard until lunchtime?"

Punishment (Again)

What if young Robert or Sherry or Dede does the wrong thing? How hard do you come down on a three, four, or five for misbehaving?

The answer lies partly with you. Your style may be to get steamed and then quickly let the steam blow out. Or you may be able to do it all with quiet insistence. Neither of these styles of handling discipline will hurt the child as long as you don't do or say things that frighten or wipe out that self-esteem. That is, you can say, "If you do that again, we'll have to skip going to the zoo." But you shouldn't say, "If you do that I'm going to tell the policeman," or, "If you do that daddy won't love you." If you must punish, be brief and to the point. Long periods of the silent treatment are much too harsh punishment for any infraction.

A few good rules of thumb at any age are:

• Don't drag out the punishment.
• Don't nag, shame, or terrify.
• Don't use language the child may take literally ("I'm going to break every bone in your body!").
• Be consistent.
• Don't have too many rules for a child to remember.

Seven Preschool Scenarios (And a Few Possible Endings)

The Foul-Mouth Disease

Five-year-old Donna has the foul-mouth disease. It's a common malady among fours and fives. Her symptoms range from calling nasty names to spouting real four-letter swear words. Her grandparents are horrified. The baby-sitter suggests the soap-in-the-mouth cure. Her parents recognize (and hope) that it's a stage. Still, they want to do something so this language doesn't get to be a habit.

Children play with words, especially as they're learning language. I've seen youngsters repeat with glee a long word— the meaning of which is lost on them. *Nematode. Fuselage. Misanthrope.* A preschooler will play with such a word, rolling it on the tongue. Of course, this sort of experimentation with words you want to encourage. On the other hand, you don't want to encourage the other kind of words. How does your youngster know the difference? Only by trial and error. So when he makes an error, you have to speak up. *You* know there's a difference between "fuselage" and "motherfucker." You have to let him know, too. Tell him exactly how you feel:

"I don't like that word. Please don't use it."

"That is not a word we use in this family."

"Susan doesn't like to be called those names. No one does."

Some families don't care about language discipline. Especially if you occasionally use X-rated language yourself, you may not want to get too firm about this one. Some parents even think it's cute. "Out of the mouths of babes," they say, pretending shock, but secretly amused. Remember, your child doesn't live in a vacuum. *You* may not care about that swear word, but the neighbors may. And Donna may get a reputation she doesn't really deserve. Purple prose coming out of a five-year-old mouth is never that attractive. If you want your child to be thought of as a desirable playmate for other children, you have to think about appropriate language. Four-letter words are not appropriate for a preschooler, and they certainly may curtail his social life. Besides, if four-letter words are part of your preschooler's vocabulary, what happens at eight or ten?

Habits

Habits. They come and go. Some seem to offend parents more than others. Most of them aren't harmful. But anything to excess is a signal. Take Sam. He pulls his hair out in little wads. Lately, it seems to be taking up a good deal of Sam's time (and leaving scabs on his scalp). His parents deduce, correctly, that something is bothering Sam. Turns out it is pressure from school. At four? That's right. Sam is in a nursery school that insists on *teaching* him numbers and letters and a lot of other things that Sam just isn't ready for. So Sam literally pulls his hair out with tension. Most habits don't get to this point. But if they do, rather than discipline the habit itself, it's wise to try to find out what's causing it.

Sex Play

Ron's mother has just walked into the playroom and found Ron and a neighbor's four-year-old naked. They seem to be playing show-and-tell with their personal parts. Ron's mother knows it's important not to punish Ron for his curiosity. On the other hand, she doesn't want him going public with it.

Ron's mother doesn't say that what he and his friend were doing was dirty or naughty. She simply tells them to put on their clothes and that she doesn't want them playing that game anymore.

Ron's parents will follow this up with a little talk about sex sometime soon. They will make it clear that they're available to answer questions. Neither of them will overdo it; preschool kids can't comprehend all the details of sex. The simpler the answers the better, as long as everything you say is true. (No babies being found under cabbage leaves, please.)

Just because Ron's parents handled this well doesn't mean sex education is easy. Many parents feel both anger and panic when they discover their small child masturbating or playing sex games. And the pressure from society about matters sexual cannot be underestimated. Neighbors and friends make it difficult for parents to be casual with their youngsters' questions about sex. And your own upbringing is bound to have an influence on how you treat your pre-schooler's first questions and experiments.

There's a good deal of latitude in the way that children can learn about sex. If your concepts of sex education lean toward the straitlaced, and you're comfortable with that, you'll have to pass those values to your children. And you should. Just make sure, whatever you do, that you don't make your offspring feel guilty and dirty.

The Gimmes

> Smiling girls, rosy boys,
> Come and buy my little toys;
> Monkeys made of gingerbread,
> And sugar houses painted red.

The gimmes is a disease that can arrive like chicken pox or mumps at this preschool age. And no child of today seems immune. In fact, this has come to be known as "the gimme generation."

Take Laura. She wants whatever her eye lights on, and she usually gets it. That's the problem: Laura has seldom been told that she can't have everything. So how is she to know?

The discipline of restraint is something all children have to learn, whether rich or poor. It's no favor to indulge a child's every wish, even if parents can afford to. On the other hand, it's not easy for Laura's dad and mom to resist those cries of, "Everyone else has an electronic game," or, "I *really* need that play oven." Nor do they like hearing, "You're a mean daddy for not getting that for me." Or even worse, seeing Laura's tears and temper when her wishes aren't gratified.

What can you say and do to discipline the gimmes?

First of all, you have to get across the message that toys and treats are special, not a "given." You can say,

"I know you want that toy. But we're not buying toys today."

or

Sorry, today is not a toy day."

or even,

We have no money for treats today."

On the other hand, if you promise a treat ("I'll bring you something when I come home") you should come through.

At some times you can say, "You may choose one thing from the toy store today."

Parents shouldn't feel guilty about monitoring their child's choice of toy. Small children are not the final arbiters of what's appropriate. If Laura picks out a twenty-five-dollar doll and you were thinking in terms of five dollars, you should speak up. One of the ways to avoid this kind of financial embarrassment with your offspring is to set limits ahead of time: "You may have a record, or a book . . ." Or, "You can pick a small stuffed animal."

Don't give in on instant gratification. The gimmes unchecked are bad for you, bad for your child, and even bad for the whole society. Remember—the child who doesn't learn to sometimes defer material gratification grows up to be the adolescent who insists on a car, who wants an unlimited college allowance, and who won't be able to handle any sort of frustration. It may even interfere with school performance. The latest research shows that youngsters who are used to having every wish gratified don't do as well in school as those who have a more realistic view of what they can and can't have.

Manners

Manners are learned partly by example. Five-year-old Ted knows the basics of politeness, his playmate Sheila doesn't. Is it because Ted is "better" or "smarter"? Not really. But Ted's parents have made a point of being polite. They press for manners and are a model for the behavior that Ted is beginning to copy. For instance, at the table in Ted's house, it's always,

"Please pass the bread."

"Thank you, Ted."

"Excuse me. I didn't mean to interrupt you."

In addition, Ted's folks occasionally reinforce a manners rule.

"Ted, you need to take the first piece of carrot that you touch."

"Let's hold the elevator button so that Mrs. Carter can get the baby carriage out."

Sheila's folks don't do any of this. Maybe they think Sheila will learn manners later, through some mysterious process that's not connected with their input.

She won't. And it will be harder to discipline manners later on. What's cute at three, four, five, will be rude at six, seven, eight, and downright antisocial at ten and up.

So, yes, the discipline of manners is important. And parents are right to care about it. If Ted grouses about the fact that he must mind his manners, but Sheila doesn't have to, his parents can simply say, "Well, that's the way we do things in this house."

Children like to be polite because it makes grown-ups like them.

It's sound discipline to feed this self-image, especially if it makes life more pleasant for everyone around.

When Bedtime Is a Bad Time

If you were to make a graph of the complaints of parents in various areas of discipline, sleep problems would zoom off the chart. There's no one single answer for the sleepytime blues. As we've said earlier, some kids are better sleepers than others. But beyond that fact, sleep problems occur with all children from time to time and have to be dealt with.

Three-year-old Aaron, for instance, is a wanderer. He'll go to bed and to sleep and then wake at midnight to stalk the halls and raid the refrigerator. Aaron will get over it, but in the meantime mom and dad ought to make sure there's nothing dangerous around that Aaron can get into. (Make sure the doors are locked.) If midnight wanderers make you nervous, you can insist that Aaron stay in his room if he gets up. But leave a few interesting books and games around for him to look at. Don't lock the door; it's dangerous.

Four-year-old Dorrie is going through a period of waking at night and needing company. This is always tough to handle. Should you give in to the pleas to come into your bed? If your child seems truly distressed and if it doesn't get to be a habit, why not? Here again, you've got a line on your own child. If she's the type that will quickly get into a habit, better not to start.

Drs. Ilg and Ames, in the book *Child Behavior*, suggest that giving a four-year-old her own bed goes a long way toward easing night-waking problems. In fact, you can sometimes plant an idea. "When you have your own big bed, you won't get out of bed in the night anymore."

Five-year-olds often have really bad nightmares. You can never punish or spank, or even laugh nightmares away, and you shouldn't try. The best course is to be soothing and concerned. Often the child won't remember the dream the next morning. But she will remember your reassurances.

Bedwetting

In the nineteenth century they used to prescribe eating the testicles of a rabbit for it. Or the petals of a chrysanthemum. What's the malady? Bedwetting.

Sleep and bedwetting can be linked. A child may fall asleep, wet the bed involuntarily, and wake up. Often tears or screams accompany the realization that the fickle body that behaved so well during the day has delivered a double cross while the youngster wasn't looking.

It's normal for some children who are perfectly dry during the day to lag in their bladder control during the night. It's no fun for Julie and Johnny to wake up wet. They want, at this age, to discipline themselves to nature's call. It's heavy for mom and dad, too, since they've adjusted quickly to a small fry who's dry. So nobody's happy with the sopping mattress at midnight. Small wonder that tempers on all sides are short.

How do you handle it?

First of all, you have to realize that it is what it is called— an accident. So there's nothing to be gained by blaming. Nor by telling Julie and Johnny that they're *naughty,* or *babies,* or that they'll have to change the bed themselves or stay wet. None of that will move the situation forward. And that's what you're after.

So start by changing the clothes and the bed. Be cheerful while you're doing it. Meanwhile, assure the bedwetter it will all come out in the wash. This *doesn't* mean that you have to indicate approval. In fact, you might tell Julie that you're going to help her in her effort to stay dry.

You can help by taking Julie on a trip to the bathroom at night before you go to sleep. Be sure you get her agreement on this, otherwise she may resent being awakened.

You ought to eliminate that good-night bottle if you haven't done so already. It isn't the extra eight ounces of liquid that does John in, it may simply be the babyish pattern of bottle, sleep, urinate. That's what you want to break at this point.

Put a flannel-covered rubber pad on Julie's bed. Tell her that you're doing it to protect the mattress until she can control her bladder. It may help her to feel less anxious about her lack of control.

Some doctors say boys are more likely to be bedwetters than girls. But most of them get over it sooner or later. If "later" is too much later, and gets on your nerves, check it out with your pediatrician. Julie's or Johnny's "runs" may be physical. Don't look for psychological causes until you've looked at everything else and given the situation lots of time to solve itself.

Above all, try not to allow bedwetting—this one small aspect of your child's behavior—to become the cause of wrangling, nagging, screaming, or physical punishment. Don't send Julie or Johnny off to nursery school or kindergarten upset by a "scene." It won't help and it could actually slow down the process of attaining bladder control.

One more thought—parents often differ sharply in their approaches to bedwetting. Dad may be relaxed about it, Mom may be uptight. You could start out focusing on bedwetting and end up in a bang-up argument with each other.

Bedwetting is a touchy subject. It's important to keep cool about it. And two cool heads are better than one.

Right and Wrong

Up to now, your child's notion of right and wrong has been extremely primitive. What's right for me is *right,* has been his understanding. But now, along with other maturing signs, comes the beginning of something we can call conscience. Make no mistake, it's not there all the time. And it doesn't get there by itself. The seeds were planted by effective discipline geared to the youngster's understanding and development.

At three, you may notice that Debby or Dan can resist that tempting cookie jar between meals because they know the *result* if they violate a no-no. They have more or less forsworn pulling the cat's tail and biting the baby for the same reason. In other words, they're learning what's allowed and what's not allowed. By four, the age of boisterousness, their misbehavior will take other forms, but they will have some sense of good and bad, right and wrong. They will have a vague understanding of the difference between lying and

telling the truth. But by the time they are five, they will be
quite clear about it.

Slowly, slowly, you are building a values system. Conscience
is creeping into the picture. Through discipline, your child
is learning to do what's right, and feeling guilty if he doesn't.
Is guilt good or bad for a child? Some guilt is good. But, like
garlic in a gourmet dish, a little bit goes a long way.

Fair Play

Fair play is an important aspect of right and wrong. More
adults seem to remember unfairness in their upbringing than
remember spanking. It's amazing how much it sticks in your
mind. One adult friend told me:

> I was about five. My little brother and I were running
> around the house. He knocked over a lamp and it
> broke. My mother looked with horror on the remains
> of her lamp, turned around, and whacked me. Hard.
> I remember bawling and yelling that it wasn't fair.
> After all, he had broken the lamp, but she hit *me*. I
> still think I was right. From my point of view, there
> was no justice.

Fairness is a value that preschoolers can understand and
relate to. And parents are the best models of this virtue that
a kid can have.

Of course fair play cuts two ways. Once you've made a
point of it, you're stuck with it. From then on, you're going
to hear, "It's not fair," or, "You're not being fair" many thousands of times over the years. Many issues will go through
the family's whole judicial court system. Never mind. It's a
small price to pay for raising a decent person.

All of us are unfair sometimes. Parents are not Solomons
of wisdom. You can only try to teach fair play and live it as
much as possible.

Sometimes fair play expresses itself not so much in the
big things, but in the small ones—like:

- Keeping your word, if at all possible.
- Treating your children equally.
- Listening to your child's side of the story.
- Being consistent about what you expect from the
  child.

· Sharing, by example.
· Encouraging empathy. You can ask a four- or five-year-old, "How do you think Joe feels when you call him names?" Or, "Do you think you're being fair?"

Preschoolers and Prejudice

Part of the concept of fairness is treating other people or other groups of people fairly. Obviously, we want our children to grow up comfortable in a changing world, and to get along with many different kinds of people. The best way to do that is to expose them early to many kinds of people and to be open about other cultures and life-styles ourselves.

My grandmother used to say, "Little pitchers have big ears." It's an old-fashioned expression, but it accurately reflects the fact that young kids pick up on the attitudes of grown-ups, as well as those of other children. You're not trying to create a four-year-old philosopher. On the other hand, you can discourage jokes, remarks, and table talk that tends to denigrate any group. And if your preschooler quotes a racial, religious, or ethnic slur that he has heard, set him straight. The bottom line, of course, is how you feel. Make sure that you're passing along positive attitudes. This cuts both ways. Don't *assume* prejudice toward your group and give your children the feeling they are always victims of injustice. Another caution: Sometimes small children ask questions or say things that mimic prejudice, but aren't prejudice. A white child can be genuinely puzzled about black skin (or vice versa). It doesn't mean racial prejudice. It just means she needs some explanations.

Respect

All along you've been building a foundation of respect. Here in the preschool years, you'll want to continue. Give respect and insist on getting it back.

For instance, there are dozens of everyday situations where you can reinforce your previous indications that there should be respect for private property:

"That's your brother's camera, and not for playing with."
or

"These flowers belong to the park. They're not for picking, just for looking."

And how about respect for privacy:

"When our bedroom door is closed, that means knock and ask to come in."

"When Ruth is in her room doing homework, she needs peace and quiet."

And respect for feelings:

"It bothers me if you interrupt when I'm on the phone. Wait until I'm finished talking. I'll try not to be too long."

"You forgot to call grandma today. Give her a ring. It makes her feel good to hear from you."

Children don't learn to be respectful overnight. You'll have to cajole, remind, insist. If the rule is important, it must be kept. If it's important to you, plug for it. If your child is disrespectful, let him or her know that you aren't happy about it.

But disciplining respect is only one part of the battle. To get it you have to give it. Unfortunately, there are dozens of ways that respect between parent and child can be undermined. And most experts agree that constant disrespect between parent and child can be a breeding ground for future delinquency.

Early Warning Signs

If your child *consistently* shows disregard and lack of respect—and if you feel that you two are not getting along, that you're being ignored, that your offspring is unusually hostile—these can be early warning signs that something is out of kilter.

Sometimes parents don't think about the fact that they may be sending the wrong message to the child. Here's a little checklist. Rate yourself by answering the following questions honestly.

1. In general, are you
   a. happy with your child as he is?
   b. unhappy, and would you prefer a child who looked and/ or behaved differently?
2. Do you more often
   a. praise and compliment your child?
   b. criticize, belittle, and point out your child's weaknesses?

3. More often than half of the time, are you
   a. cuddling, tender, and pleasant?
   b. yelling, nagging, or spanking?
4. Do you usually
   a. listen to your child's questions and comments?
   b. tend to ignore them because you're busy and they're not important?
5. In the presence of other adults, do you
   a. introduce your child, include her in the general conversation, and in other ways acknowledge her presence?
   b. interrupt, ignore, shame, or ridicule her?

If your answers tended to fall into the "a" sections, you're in good shape, respect-wise. And you're on firm ground when you ask for respect from your preschooler. But if you are more in the "b" group, you may have to rethink your approach. And if you're between "a" and "b," you're still giving your youngster less than she deserves.

Different Dos and Don'ts

Talk may make discipline easier. But society is going to make it tougher. From now on, there will be other people in the discipline picture. Besides a parent or parents, and/or a housekeeper or baby-sitter or grandparents, there may be nursery school teachers, and older siblings. There are friends and friends' parents. Don't think that a preschool child doesn't notice that different people dish out dos and don'ts in different portions. There's no way you can keep your youngster from comparing the differing discipline ways of the world. Now that he is getting out more, you're not going to be the only discipline game in town, the way you were when he was in the playpen and the playroom.

This puts you on your mettle in several ways. Your ideas will begin to be held up to the glass of comparison, a process that will more or less dog your discipline efforts up to and including adolescence. Be sure that your Jack or Joan is going to try on other ideas for size. They'll try to figure out the general rules, but they may make up some of their own. They may break their own rules after they make them and may even try some of their friends' rules. There's a world of choices out there. Your boy or girl will be working hard the next few years learning what they are.

Chapter 5
School Discipline

Little Bob Snooks was fond of his books,
And loved by his usher and master;
But naughty Jack Spry, he got a black eye,
And carries his nose in a plaster.

A New Era

If you were to ask a group of children five and six what the biggest event in their lives is, most of them would not hesitate to answer *school*. Real school, they would hasten to explain. Because kids see clearly that nursery or play school or the day-care center is different from the kind of school "big kids" go to beginning at around age five.

School is the beginning of a new era, accompanied by a widening of the child's whole world. It's also the beginning of a new era for parents. There goes your "baby"—down the driveway or into the elevator, onto the school bus and out of reach of your gaze, your influence, and your discipline for six hours a day. Never again will things be just the same.

It's a significant moment. Some parents cry. Some are relieved to have young Jack or Joan out of the house from nine to three, but may feel guilty about it. A few parents say, *Good,* now let the teacher worry.

But the majority of mothers and fathers still do the worrying themselves. Will Jack do well? Will he bring disgrace on us by misbehaving or not learning or making problems for the teacher? Will Joan get a good teacher? Will the school do as good a job as I'm doing?

All parents have some of these reactions, tinted (and sometimes tainted) by recall of their own school experiences. These fragments of memory can, and often do, alter adult perceptions of what a child may be feeling. At such times, it's wise for mom and dad to remember that your kid isn't you. Whatever your feelings when your child goes off to school, rest assured you're not alone in them. It's natural for parents both to welcome the freedom that school provides and be

81

concerned that a child be able to cope well in the new environment.

Starting with Honey

The ancient Hebrews used to spread honey on a child's first alphabet. The children were permitted to lick the letters so that they would always associate reading with pleasure. This is a pretty direct way to reinforce the joy of learning. But there are many other ways in which a modern parent can deliver the same message.

- Act as if school and learning are important and your child will think they're important.
- Show respect for teachers and your youngster will mirror that respect.
- Believe that schools are places of fun as well as work and your kid will believe it.
- See to it that your youngster has a quiet place for study; this delivers the message that school has value.
- Be a model for the idea that one has to *work* in order to attain certain goals. (You can't get something for nothing, especially learning.)

And one more often neglected idea—it's crucial that parents not only get across the idea that school is worthy, but that it's *compulsory* for all children.

This may seem very simple and basic, but many children don't catch on to it right away. A child may look forward to school as an exciting new experience that the "older kids" have. But she may be quite sure she can stop going whenever she wants to. A child needs to get into the frame of mind that there are no two ways about it. As Dr. Benjamin Spock says in his famous book on child care, "The seven-year-old who is nervous about going to school is made more secure when his father reminds him that he has to go anyway."

Rule Days

Schools expect children to know how to do certain things by the time they're school age. The rules vary from community

to community. In general, your youngster will be expected
to dress himself, keep track of his clothes, carry papers and/
or a lunchbox to and from school. He'll be expected to listen
and follow instructions. He may be expected to sit quietly
for varying amounts of time (sometimes perceived as too
long by the average five- or six-year-old).

Some school systems assume that a youngster knows the
alphabet when she enters the first grade. Some count on the
child's being able to write her name or to recognize colors or
count to ten. These expectations, more custom than law,
may be arbitrary and you may have to give your offspring
an assist in coping with them.

What do you do if knowing the alphabet is expected in
your local school and *Sesame Street* didn't quite rub off on
your five? One of the best things you can do is find out about
it early on. Then you can respond in any number of ways.
You may not want to spend the summer teaching the alphabet yourself. You may not think it's crucial. But you could
have an alphabet chart around. Say casually that the alphabet is one of the things she's going to learn in school and
that some of the kids may already have learned it. This way
the child can decide whether she wants to learn now and
play later, or the reverse. You don't want her to be unhap-
pily surprised come September. It could be pretty stressful
to go into a class of strangers and discover that you're the
only one who doesn't know her Ps and Qs.

You should certainly try to visit school well before your
youngster starts. Many schools now give kindergarten kids
and first-graders a chance to see classes in action the spring
before they start school. In other schools, teachers meet with
parents and kids at an "open house." And some good teachers call their young students on the phone to introduce
themselves.

If some of this friendly "prep" for operation school is missing in your school district, make it happen. Call the school
and introduce yourself. Ask for a preschool interview with
your child's teacher or to see a class in action. It's one way
to get across the idea that you favor the school and the home
working together for education.

Starting Time

Starting school is one of the times when family disciplines
already set up can help. Let's face it: Every parent knows
that it's usually easier to send number-two child off to start

school than it was to send number one. Why? Because number two has already seen big brother or sister going off. Can he do less than follow in his sibling's footsteps? Also the parent has gone through one separation successfully. The second one usually goes more smoothly.

It's good discipline for both younger and older child to have them both involved in the younger sibling's starting school. It's good for the big guy because he can feel important. He knows the ropes, can help, can reassure. It's good for the younger child because he has a model. He sees that brother or sister goes off to that big brick building with reasonable calm, so he might as well. He wants to play by the rules since he has seen them acted out. It's good for you as a parent because it makes it easier. Often you already know the school system and can prepare your younger child.

One word of caution: Every child is different. Your older child can open many doors for your younger one, but he can also close a few without meaning to. If the first kid in school is bright and a leader and does everything super well, that doesn't mean that number two has to live up to that. Teachers who compare can make it difficult for number twos. So can parents. Don't.

There's a good deal of tension associated with starting school. Under the strain some behavior that you haven't seen for a long while may come back. Bed-wetting, nightmares, upset stomachs, headaches, tears, or temper tantrums—one or more may make an appearance. Jack may seem more tired than usual, Joan more wild. What do you do about it? In practical terms, the first week or two of school is a particularly important time to be supportive, loving, and cheerful. Don't raise issues if you can avoid it. No bombshells. Understanding and reassurance will generally help matters much more than toughness. In other words—a little "honey."

As your child settles in, keep an eye on what's going on. Praise work he brings home. Encourage newly acquired skills. Get familiar with what he's learning and see to it that he gets some time to practice the concept. Take the time to play games that reinforce number and word concepts. Around the house, show him how these concepts are used in everyday ways.

"How many slices of bread are left, Dan?"

"How many sandwiches can we make with four slices?"

"Can you help me make a sign for the grass that says *Keep Off*?"

"Want to help me with the grocery list? I'll help you spell the words."

Junior Achieving

Come hither, then, good little boy,
And learn your alphabet,
And then a pair of boots and spurs
Like papa's you shall get.

Giving your child a helping hand with numbers or reading is fine. But make sure the helping hand doesn't turn into too hard a shove toward achievement.

We all know it's a competitive world. In many ways, a six-year-old begins to deal with this fact of life when he gets into school. But he's not old enough to handle too much adult pressure. Sometimes parents forget this in the rush toward achievement. And you get the odd picture of a child of barely seven being groomed to get into a "good" college. Or you hear the parent of a five-year-old talking about hiring a math tutor. If parent expectations get out of line with the age and maturity of the child, it could spell trouble. Achievement-oriented discipline isn't healthy for the little citizen who is trying to find his way in a new place with confusing new rules, just at a time when he's most rigid. School has enough built-in pressure for the six-, seven-, and even eight-year-old. It's far better for a youngster if parents can ease up on some of those achievement expectations, instead of encouraging them with competitive statements like:

"You got four A's and a B? How come you got a B?"

Discipline should not be used to make school the bad guy:

"Just wait until you get to school. They'll shape you up."

Or:

"That's no way for a first-grader to act."

It's important to develop healthy attitudes toward school. Discipline should help, not hobble, learning.

Some Dos and Don'ts

> • Do share learning discoveries like reading and writing whenever possible.

- Encourage budding skills.
- Praise your young scholar whenever possible.
- Lend a hand if you can with school projects that require parent involvement.
- Don't give the impression that you're always testing what she knows. No one likes to be on the spot all the time, least of all a child struggling to decode those mysterious squiggles and lines that someone has said are words and numbers.
- Never shame or ridicule a youngster for what she doesn't know.
- Try not to compare your child to her classmates or the neighbor's child or even her own brothers and sisters. If you do, you're going to discourage learning—just the opposite of the effect you're after.

School Problems

Most children settle into the school routine well, after some ups and downs. But once in a while, problems do occur. Here are a few that may sound familiar.

Danny just won't sit still in school. He runs around the classroom and drives the teacher crazy. He has no interest in reading or doing ditto sheets. The only thing he likes is the playground.

Debby is afraid of the teacher. She says the teacher screams. Debby isn't used to that. The rest of the kids don't seem to mind. Is she too sensitive?

The school says Alan is a slow learner, but I never noticed that at home. I think they're blaming my child for their failure.

Gina is very bright. She knows how to read already. That's why she's giving the teacher a hard time.

The teacher says Roger is an angel in school. But he's awful at home.

The teacher says Eileen is a hellion in school. That's funny; she's fine at home.

The teacher says George gets too upset if his paper isn't perfect. What's wrong with trying to be the best?

All of these are everyday situations that come up among children, teachers, and parents. Each of them may be a minor problem *at this stage*. But they could turn into whopping big ones if they aren't taken care of. Some of them are related to discipline. Some of them may be related to different routines and standards in school. The important message here is that you can't drop the lines of communication when you drop your kid at the bus stop.

Listen to what your child is saying. Every kid complains about school and about teachers. But some complaints last longer than others and some have more of a ring of urgency to them. That's why it's important to tune up your ears. If your youngster is really bothered about something that's going on in school, it's worth a phone call.

What if the school calls you?

"Daniel is disruptive." Or, "Lara has a learning problem." Or, "Andrea is always crying."

It's hard to react well to a certain kind of school phone call.

Many parents rush to defend their chicks, which is good instinct, but may not be the best thing for your offspring in the long run. If a teacher calls you, it's very worthwhile to listen to what she says, rather than trying the case and giving the verdict off the top of your head. Sure, some teachers have been known to be wrong. On the other hand—teachers don't have your hang-ups about your son or daughter. And they have an overview that comes from seeing hundreds of kids. Maybe they can see something that you missed.

The best way for parents and teachers to work is *together*. Parents should support teachers whenever they can. Teachers should do likewise with parents. The two can form a support network for the best interests of your child.

How does discipline fit into this home-school framework? Very often discipline problems show up in school. For instance, George, who gets upset when his paper isn't perfect, may be subject to too much discipline at home. He's being pressured to do well so much that he's afraid to make one little mistake. Or take Roger, who behaves well only in school. Roger may need the firm limits of his school situation. He doesn't have enough limits at home.

One of the most useful aspects of school may be that, as a parent, you can get a broader perspective on your child by seeing her in this new setting, interacting with a number of other kids her age.

Whatever happens in school, you should lend an ear if there appear to be clouds on the horizon. Now's the time, before they develop into a storm.

Good Timing

A diller, a dollar, a ten o'clock scholar,
What makes you come so soon?
You used to come at ten o'clock
And now you come at noon.

Children in the primary grades are apt to need help in organizing their time and their efforts. Dawdlers, oversleepers, and frantic last-minute rushers will all be under considerable pressure from school scheduling. The earlier they learn, the easier it will be for them and for you.

Teach your six-year-old to be responsible for waking up in good time to get ready for school. Sometimes an alarm clock of one's own turns the trick. But sometimes even that isn't enough to drag a reluctant hibernator from under winter covers. You can't act as a second alarm clock forever. Nor can you always drive tardy touslehead to school when she has missed the bus. Obviously, what is needed here is a schedule. If you see that it is taking all too long for your youngster to dress and eat and get out the door on school days, then it's time for a little scheduling.

First of all, agree on an earlier alarm setting.

Second, try getting some things ready the night before. Lay out clothes, lunch money, or lunch box. The hassle in our family used to be about making lunch until we discovered that many sandwiches can be made in advance and frozen. The important aspect of these night-before decisions is to make the choices stick. No last-minute changes of mind or wardrobe.

Try to anticipate. "Got your papers? How about your note?" The trick here is for you to help the child learn to remember, *not* to play permanent backup position.

Insist your child allow time for breakfast (and don't skip breakfast yourself). Most nutritionists agree that breakfast is the most important meal of the day, so try to hold the line on this one. You can sometimes create new respect for breakfast if you offer unbreakfast foods—soup, egg salad, grilled cheese are all good foods. Who's to say they can't be eaten at breakfast?

What part does a good stick-to-the-ribs breakfast and discipline start to play in school success? Here's a real-life example that may provide an answer.

Donna gets up late. As usual. Half dressed, she bolts out the front door without breakfast, barely making the bus. After she's on the bus, she discovers that she has dropped her homework. Now she's scared. That paper was supposed to be brought back. For the rest of the school day, Donna is in a school *daze*. She hardly hears the lesson because she's worrying about that lost paper. By eleven o'clock she's half asleep because she hasn't had anything to eat. The fog persists until lunchtime. The morning has been a waste.

In the afternoon, the teacher calls for the papers. Donna tells her tale of woe. The teacher is not understanding, and Donna is embarrassed in front of her peers. But after all, the plain truth is that this youngster did not fulfill her responsibility. So Donna has had a bad day. And too many bad days like this will add up to school problems for Donna.

Let's see how a little discipline might change this picture and save the day for Donna.

To begin with, someone in the family acts as enforcer for wake-up time. It could be an older child, a parent, or even a housekeeper. Donna is given one or two warning calls:

"Five minutes to breakfast, Donna."

Or:

"By the time you're finished brushing your hair, breakfast will be on the table."

And then one other reminder:

"Did you check the list we made last night?"

The point is, a child needs help in getting herself together. If you see the lunch box standing on the table and the child is going out the door, there's no harm in reminding. *On the other hand,* if time after time the act, instead of getting together, is falling on its face, you're going to have to step back and let Donna take the consequences. She may have to miss the bus and be late, with whatever that entails.

On the cheerful side, with a little encouragement most youngsters learn the basics of organization quickly. A few weeks of reminders and they're in the groove. In fact, the primary-grader's love of "rules" may propel him into so much organization you'll be floored! Some six- and seven-year-olds will remind a parent about signing a paper fifty times.

But remember that what you do is as important as what you say. If your house is a zoo before school time, take a closer look at how much is your own lack of organization. If the whole scene has gotten out of hand, you and your spouse will have to exercise a little self-discipline to get things back on the track.

School Cheating

One of the things that may come up in school is cheating. You could get a note from the teacher saying that your pride and joy has been copying a friend's ditto sheet or allowing her eyes to stray to a neighbor's page during tests.

Where did I go wrong? you wonder. Maybe nowhere. Let's see.

It may be the kind of cheating that surfaces because the six-year-old's understanding of the rules is still wobbly. It's not an easy thing to understand, this cheating business. What is cheating, anyhow? Why is it okay to copy from the chalkboard, but not okay to copy from your neighbor? And why is it okay to learn what the right answer is, as long as you don't learn it from a friend?

Children need to understand cheating before they can be expected to refrain from doing it. Both school and home have to be clear about the rules. One youngster expressed his sound definition of cheating this way:

"It's like taking someone else's lunch."

Of course, understanding doesn't always guarantee that cheating is over with. A six-, seven-, or even eight-year-old may still cheat, as a matter of expediency. There are several ways to handle cheating. Sometimes it helps to be direct: "Okay, Julian, I'll play another game with you—but only if you don't cheat." Or, you might even say: "Look, you lost this game, but you won the last one. You can't win all the time."

It's not necessary to deliver a long lecture on losing gracefully (nor will your offspring understand it). The important thing to get across is that losing can be tolerated and that cheating is not the way to play the game.

Cheating may, however, take another form. Erica, a young scholar, was given a short homework assignment. She was supposed to bring to school some information about beavers. But the beaver assignment took a back seat to the great program on TV and then to playing at her girlfriend's house. Time ran out. So, with a maximum of nerve (and a minimum of deviousness), Erica lifted her girlfriend's beaver material. It didn't take long for the teacher to discover the word-for-word duplicate and to figure out which was the original. And to chastise the offender.

In this kind of situation, parents need to deal with the cheating another way, by actions rather than words. Some help in organizing time seems to be the ticket here. Helping children to see the value in a little delayed gratification (which would have allowed Erica time to do her beaver homework) is one of the first steps to learning the most important kind of discipline—self-discipline.

School Food

Some kids put their feet down hard about school lunches. They'll swear that poisonous messes are conjured in the cafeteria. They will *never* eat that stuff, they vow.

Usually, school lunches are not nearly so bad as your young connoisseur would have you believe. Sometimes kids can't adjust, at first, to both the idea of school *and* eating strange food in a strange place. If you don't mind your kid brown-bagging it, then by all means do it, at least for a while. But if preparing lunch presents a problem for you, you'd better try to get your child to accept school lunches.

First of all, check them out. Visit the cafeteria and see what the complaints are about. If the pizza and the Jell-O are at least a "B" on your culinary report card, you should press a bit.

It's not bad here to make a deal. Start with eating at the cafeteria one day a week. Then raise it to two. Don't fall for threats that Jack won't eat. The point is, if the food is good and if the cafeteria is more convenient for you, it can be negotiated. Nowhere is it written that everything should be for the child's convenience.

The other thing to realize is that kids will often eat things at school that they won't eat at home. But they won't tell you. So don't be too concerned about whether your youngster is eating; children seldom go hungry for long.

Latchkey Kids

Here am I, little Billy Bone,
When nobody's with me, I'm always alone.

After children get into all-day school, many mothers go back to work. This timing has a certain amount of logic behind it. The child will now be away from home for most of the day anyway, the parents reason.

And so arrangements are made for "pick up" or for someone to care for the child for the few hours between the end of the school day and the time that mom or dad finishes work. In some families an older sibling, a neighbor, or grandparents take up the slack when a parent is working. Some people have housekeepers or sitters. Others have parents whose work hours are flexible enough so they can be home to greet the returning student.

But in about four million homes, according to the latest count, kids are given a key to the house. They're on their own from the time school is over until the time that one parent or the other gets home from work. These moms and dads know that it isn't an ideal solution to the two-payroll household, but for them there is simply no other way to work things out.

Single-Parent Problems

Single parents have it even tougher. They usually have to cope with the latchkey problem alone, and often it begins when their children are quite young. Whichever parent has custody of the children, the juggling of time schedules, work life, and school life becomes a major factor in the bringing up of children. And the kids of single parents have to cope in hundreds of ways with the subtle message that their family may be "different."

"Take this note home to your *parents*."

"Tell a story about what your mommy and daddy do at home."

Outside of the fortunate few households where money is no object, any working parent is inevitably under stress. He or she has to hold down a job and hold up the responsibility of being a parent. It's not easy. And it's no wonder that a single parent in this situation occasionally works on a short fuse. Said one mother:

> I can handle it as long as nothing goes wrong. But if Eileen gets a cold and has to stay home from school, then I'm in trouble. I start phoning around like a maniac and often, in my area, there's no one home to sit with her. So either I have to take a day off from work and lose pay or I have to take a chance and leave her alone. Then I worry all day at work.

Or here's a father who is a single parent:

> I sometimes get resentful that I have the total responsibility of caretaker for our children. I used to think we could share it. But my ex is so unreliable. I called her once when I had to go out of town to a meeting. She was two hours late and the kids were in a panic. I never tried that again.

The Latchkey Life: Hard on Kids

On the kids' side, it's hard to come home to an empty house. Sometimes kids need instant talk, or comfort, and they can't get it if no one is home. Most often they "get over" what is bothering them, but once in a while something important is missed. That's why it's good if working parents can make time in the evening for a little "heart-to-heart" talk time, so that problems get aired.

Sometimes children resent their parents' absence, partic-ularly if it comes after a long period when they had a parent at home. The resentment can take the form of moping, or beating up on a little sister, or misbehaving in school. Other times it can be quite direct:

"Why do you have to work? Johnny's mother doesn't work." Or:

"You're always leaving us. I don't want you to go to work."

It's necessary for parents and their children to have a clear understanding about the "why" of the latchkey situa-tion. Kids can be enormously resourceful and cooperative when they can see the reasons for them to be. They even react well to quite adverse situations, if they fully under-stand the problem. What children *don't* like is uncertainty. Not knowing who'll pick them up after school, or *if* they'll have a sitter, is often harder for them to cope with than knowing they'll have to go home alone. And a no-show parent is far worse than a latchkey!

Latchkey Discipline

There's nothing wrong with telling your child, in a matter-of-fact way, why you're working. Is it because the family needs the money? Then say so. Is it because you have skills you need to use, or because it gives you satisfaction? These are good and valid reasons, too. Whatever you do, don't tie your working to your child's behavior.

If you say:

"I'm working because you're so bad I have to get away from you."

Or:

"You want so many things that I have to get more money." That's not an explanation—that's taking the kid on a guilt trip!

The latchkey life also requires that certain important rules be in place.

First and foremost your child should know exactly what to do and where to go after school. If a sitter is waiting at home, the youngster should report home every day without fail. If an older child is in charge, both children should thoroughly understand what they're supposed to do. They should have practiced the routine under your supervision.

Your child should know at least two telephone numbers to call in case of an emergency. One of them should be the number at your place of work or your spouse's. The other should be a dependable friend or relative who is apt to be available.

Whether your child can handle these basics will clue you in as to whether he or she is mature enough to be left alone. Many five- and six-year-olds simply aren't. You'll have to be the best judge of that.

One of my children was decidedly a dreamer at six. I remember once being on a crowded subway and seeing him about to walk off, clutching the coat of a perfect stranger. He was busy gazing at the subway signs and thought he was hanging on to me!

On the basis of my own experience, I don't think that most six-year-olds should be left at home without some sort of supervision. Even with some sevens it can be risky. Eight is the lowest age I would leave a youngster unsupervised in a house or apartment, and in some neighborhoods I would raise the age to nine. If the family budget permits, I'd hire a competent sitter or family daycare mother or I'd try to swap or trade childcare with a neighbor. But what if you can do none of the above?

Personal Safety Rules

Then you'll have to depend on discipline and it will have to be strict, no-nonsense rules. You should agree on them with your child or children and also agree that they are non-negotiable. For instance, here's a minimum list of nevers (and make it clear that you mean *never*):

- Never go anywhere with a stranger, no matter what kind of story he/she tells you. (You might even play-act this one: "Supposing he says so-and-so, or . . .")
- Never open the door of the apartment or house for *anyone* except those people you've specifically been told you can let in.
- Never use matches or play with fire.
- Never play with knives or other sharp instruments or dangerous weapons. (Here's a good time to childproof your house!)
- Never take any medicine when no one is home.
- Never change your routine (birthday party, after-school game) without letting your parent know where you are. The same thing goes for the parent.

Naturally, you can't think of everything. And you don't want to give your kid so many warnings that she'll be a nervous wreck by the time you come home. What you can do is anticipate life-threatening situations within reason and make strong rules about them. But discipline isn't only "don'ts" and "nevers." If you give your child responsibilities that you know she can handle, and then praise her for handling them, you'll be molding a strong young person capable of coping with the unusual.

One parent proudly tells the story of her eight-year-old who was caught in the New York City blackout of a few years ago. The youngster was on her way to a music lesson. She stopped at a store to buy candles, and then walked up twelve flights of stairs to her music teacher's home, where she stayed until she was picked up. When asked about her actions, she coolly said that she had reasoned that her teacher might need candles and that she had decided to stay there because her teacher was an older person and might welcome her company. And because she knew her parents would look for her there. This is the kind of reasoning that you want to cultivate through positive discipline.

And keep in touch. A call from the office to make sure your kid is home will make both you and your child feel more secure.

Working parents worry about their kids and it puts additional stress on them. The best way to cope with this added dose of worry is to firm up the rules and go off to work knowing that your youngster is disciplined enough to follow them.

Solutions to the Latchkey Life

Are you locked in by a latchkey situation? You may not have to be. More and more, parents are sitting down with schools to devise ways in which kids can have structure and supervision for the time between the end of school and the end of the work day. These after-school programs are usually started by moms and dads. And they're good—for lots of reasons. The main one is that they lift a ton of worry off parental shoulders. For another, kids love them. In a number of programs, the children of nonworking parents have been included, at the kids' request.

But the biggest fringe benefit of after-school groups is that they generally bring school and home together in closer cooperation than is usually possible in the regular school curriculum. Parents are often the initiators of the programs. Youngsters, too, can help to plan what activities are going to go on. All of this cooperative activity is bound to help build a sense of community.

What you need to get an after-school program together is the will to replace the latchkey with something better. Take a look at community programs in your area. If there's another after-school program going, you can use it as a model and point of reference when you go to your own school board. A local parent group may help put you in touch with ongoing activities.

No working parent has to be told that the latchkey life is difficult for both parent and child. Supervising a youngster from the office or factory is stressful. A supervised after-school group, set up in the public school or in a community center, may be one way you can both take the pressure off and provide a caring, structured environment for your school-age child.

Six to Nine: The Middle Years

Manners in the dining room,
Manners in the hall,
If you don't behave yourself
You shan't have any at all.

One of the greatest contributions to the cause of discipline has been systematic research on the behavior of children. The Gesell Institute, one of the leaders in this field, has been collecting data on what kids do at various ages for a long time. They can now tell parents pretty much what to expect from a youngster from birth to adolescence. This information is decidedly valuable, besides being downright reassuring. For example, the parent whose seven-year-old has been caught filching coins from mama's handbag can be comforted by knowing that this is one typical seven-year-old stunt. The knowledge doesn't prevent dealing with the behavior, but it does give a parent a sense that other parents have similar problems.

So before we tackle discipline among the middle years, let's dip into some of that literature on six-, seven-, and eight-year-old behavior and see what the predictions are. Keep in mind that no two children are exactly alike (as no two adults are alike). Don't look for typical behavior to necessarily start on the dot of your six-, seven-, or eight-year-old's birthday. It may appear later. Or not at all. These are simply *general* patterns of behavior in the middle years.

Sassy Six

First the bad news. Stubborn. Fresh. Negative. Babyish. Some or all of this unlovely list may describe your six-year-old. You may need to hold on to your sense of humor. Because six has been known to cheat at games, resort to extremely babyish behavior and give mother (especially) a very hard time.

99

This is what you may hear from a six-year-old:

"I hate you, Mommy."

"I don't love you anymore." (Variation on "You don't love me anymore.")

"She didn't play fair. I *won!*" (Tears and temper at losing.)

"Yucch! I'm not eating that macaroni again!"

Or

"Why can't I have macaroni again?"

Six has been described as a case of walking growing pains.

Poor six. So at odds with himself. You can see indecision written all over him. So he reverses himself, agonizes over decisions, flips back and forth until a poor parent is driven to the edge.

Nor does first grade make things easier for six. All of a sudden, he's smack in the middle of a new situation where he knows nothing. He's starting from scratch.

But is this the whole story? Does a parent have to look forward only to a year of conflict with six? Not at all. Six will delight you with his giddy pride of accomplishment—whether it's a learning discovery or a physical feat. And other positive signs of maturity may be just below the surface—like the leaf buds that are barely visible on a tree branch in winter. On balance, the winter of your discontent with a six-year-old may be brightened by more than an occasional thaw.

Sulky Seven

Here's Sulky Sue;
What shall we do?
Turn her face to the wall
Till she comes to.

By the age of seven, you may lose your fresh kid. But you could get a dash of sulky seven—the moody, whiny, tattling, fussy complainer. Here's some sample seven dialogue:

"That's not the right way to do it."

"Stay out of my room. Don't touch my things. Close the door; I want to be alone."

"You're not my boss."

(Weeping) "You're always picking on me."

(Whining) "Why do I always have to be the one to take out the garbage?"

"I'm going to tell on you. Ms. Gilbert, Johnny copied."

On the other hand, any profile of a seven-year-old has to acknowledge the fact that she has come a long way in the area of competency. You see initiative and a love of logic. There's a real awareness of others, even though it may be spotty. At seven, you can sometimes get a real idea of the adult to come. Which is why someone has said, "That which she is at seven, she will be at seventy."

On the other hand, you wouldn't want to think that your child will be as unhappy as she often seems to be at seven. Never fear. That all-too-frequent frown will most probably be replaced by a smile by age eight.

Energetic Eight

Eight has come so far from six and seven that it is almost impossible to do a word portrait of him. About all you can say is that eight is full of contradictions.

He is driven to excel, but he has no persistence (except perhaps in practicing sports).

He has a strong conscience but he still tells lies, as a practical matter.

He is brave and daring, but very often pushes to do things way beyond his capabilities.

He has almost a compulsion to be part of the group.

Here are some of the things you may hear from a typical eight-year-old:

"Why can't I go downtown by myself? I can handle it. I'm not a baby."

"I'll finish mowing the rest of the lawn later."

"Yes, I did tell the kids we have a vacation house. Everyone has a vacation house, that's why."

If there's any age when parents have to be both liberators and trainers, it's with age eight. For eight is on the cusp. He's already practicing some self-discipline. But he still needs parental guidance (even though he may try to reject it).

These are general pictures of what to expect at six, seven, and eight. But how do these traits show up in the ordinary everyday life of parent and child? And what do you do about them? Here are some common discipline problems and suggestions as to how to cope.

Cheating

Taffy was a Welshman,
Taffy was a cheat,
Taffy came to my house
And stole a piece of meat.

It's a fact. Most kids in this age group cheat. They hate to lose so much that they'll do almost anything to win, from the most transparent ploy to the most devious shenanigans. Listen to a group of sixes and sevens playing a game. Even if they don't actually cheat, it's obvious that not one of them can lose gracefully. What a crew of soreheads!

You certainly don't want your child to win by cheating. And yet, if it's a stage, you wonder whether just letting it blow over might not be the answer.

Better not. There are several more useful things you can do. The first might be to go easy for a while on the competitive games in the family. One set of parents I spoke with noticed that their six-year-old was particularly competitive with dad. In their nightly game of checkers, the daughter couldn't stand having her father beat her all the time and invariably resorted to ill-concealed cheating. The dad toyed with the idea of letting the youngster win. But, in truth, that doesn't solve it—for two reasons. First of all, the child very soon catches on to what you're doing. And second, you're creating a very artificial situation. In this case, the father and daughter agreed not to play at all for a while. They resumed their games a few years later when losing wasn't such a heavy burden for the youngster.

What do you do when several children are playing a board game and a fracas erupts because of *your* youngster's cheating? You may have to step in and show your youngster that he's behaving abominably. Especially if you actually see the cheating, you'll have to confront it, and indicate to your child that it's not the way the game is played. If you can keep your youngster from getting angry, it would be helpful. Kids really hate to be humiliated in front of their friends, even if they know very well that the parents are right. So spare the public lectures, but make it clear that you know that the counter in that parcheesi game was moved.

What about the parent who says, "All the kids cheat. Why make a big issue out of it? He'll outgrow it."

How can he outgrow it if no one tells him it's wrong?

To discipline cheating, you have to say that it's wrong. Say it again and again if necessary. At the same time, you might ask yourself where the behavior is coming from. Does your child feel too much pressure to achieve? Is some of that pressure coming from your direction? Perhaps you need to get across the message that you are proud of him for trying, *whether he wins or loses.*

The Bottom Line

Do: Speak out against cheating and discuss it with your youngster.

Do: Cheerfully (but firmly) refuse to play a game with the child who cheats. If siblings complain about the cheater, tell them to refuse to play, too.

Do: Provide models of parents who are square-shooters.

Don't: Constantly set up situations that force the child into a win-or-lose position.

Don't: Encourage cheating by putting a lot of emphasis on coming in first or winning. (E.g., "How did you do in the ball game? How did Josh do? Did you do the best?")

Cheating is a phase. If it's handled properly, it will pass. But if it isn't, it could be a long-term problem.

Food

> Jack Sprat could eat no fat,
> His wife could eat no lean . . .
> And so between them both, you see,
> They licked the platter clean.

Even in the most well-ordered households, food issues rise like bread dough every once in a while. You can't ignore them and sometimes they can be mighty annoying. My children were always good eaters, but when one of them suddenly started *smelling* every piece of food I gave him, I had a hard time being civil. What I didn't know at the time was that little food quirks are common among primary-graders. Some will get a fix on one food and want to have it every day.

Others may decide that they will never again eat meat, or cereal, or whatever.

Generally, these fads come and go. Very often they're affected by what a child sees in a buddy's lunch box or hears in school. And eagerness to follow peer food fads may impel Joan to turn up her nose at your menu. I knew a youngster who was so enchanted by a school poster on food groups that she refused to eat anything that wasn't pictured there. It took quite a while before mom and dad got across the idea that these were examples of the kinds of food to eat, not the *only* foods.

Should you discipline food fads? Only if they seem to be harmful. A month or two of nothing but peanut butter and jelly is not going to do your youngster's digestive tract any great damage. A month of nothing but candy and cake or snacks is a different story.

In general, if there are a few foods that a youngster really hates, or is allergic to, it's just being considerate to make sure that when the liver (a common hate) or the spinach is served there are other things for the child to fill up on. What you don't want to do is get into the habit of catering to a whole parcel of special foods. If you have several kids and each one wants something else, you'll never get out of the kitchen.

The best response to "I don't like this" is "Then have some more of this." If there are further protests you can simply say, "This is what we're having tonight. Maybe you'll change your mind later." And take the offending food away cheerfully.

The important point here is that you try not to get agitated or annoyed. It's irritating to see good food wasted. But it's a bad idea to get into the habit of haggling over it:

"If you eat some of this you can have dessert."

Or cajoling:

"Just one more spoonful."

Or punishing:

"Now you just sit here until you finish every bite."

The Picky Eater

If your child is generally a good eater, you can offer a balanced diet and pretty much forget about food as a subject for discipline. However, if you have a poor eater at your table, you may be able to alter both your youngster's behavior and your own.

The first thing you can do is make it a rule to offer the picky one only very small portions. She can always come back for seconds, but may be discouraged by the heaping platefuls you've been dishing out.

Another thing that can help is to make sure that snacks are not appetite killers. An afternoon snack of milk and cookies is okay. Apples and cheese, raisins and nuts, are all good snack foods. But gooey packaged cakes, candy, potato chips, and soda are guaranteed to kill persnickety appetites, particularly when they're served close to mealtimes.

There's no way that you can make a delicate eater into a robust one, so don't bargain. Just resign yourself to the fact that your child is probably a normal kid who simply doesn't eat a lot.

The only discipline you can invoke is to make sure there is respect for food and the people who *do* want to eat it. You should insist on politeness at the table. No making faces! No vomiting noises! No throwing food around. And your finicky one should be willing to try a new food now and then.

Too Much

What about trouble turning the eating faucet off, rather than on?

It used to be that fat children were considered healthy children. Nowadays we know that this isn't so. Fat doesn't necessarily mean healthy. You want to encourage eating habits that will promote good health and long life.

But how? It's delicate disciplining an overeater. And anyway, overweight may not mean that Joan is overeating. But it can mean that she is eating the wrong foods. Ice cream, candy, rich cakes, all tend to put on the pounds. Discipline is not keeping those foods around to tempt. Food habits, as we talked about earlier, are family habits and everyone may have to give up the chocolate layer cake binges at home in order to help Joan. You can *all* substitute fresh fruit, skimmed milk, simple cookies. Exercise is another activity that the whole family can do together for very little cost and much benefit. One family bought a tape cassette with a series of exercises on it and they play it and do the exercises together every evening.

Never call attention to a child's overeating or weight problem in a ridiculing manner. This can be really hurtful. But if someone else brings it up, talk about it frankly.

"Donna called me fat," your Joan may report. Don't avoid the issue. Better to say, "Yes, well, you are a bit overweight. If Donna's remarks bother you, let's see how we can do something about it."

The Bottom Line

Do: Offer a variety of nutritious foods in small portions.

Do: Go light on sweet treats and greasy and fatty foods.

Do: Try to make mealtime a pleasant and relaxed time.

Do: Provide a model of good eating habits by eating well yourself (a healthy breakfast, for instance).

Don't: Keep junk food in the house.

Don't: *Make* your child eat a certain food or a certain *amount* of food.

Don't: Use food as a bribe, a punishment, or a reward.

Don't: Spend hours cooking special dishes to tempt a poor eater.

Lying

The lying of a six- or seven-year-old is different from the lying that a toddler does. The younger child doesn't really understand what he's doing. The older child does understand, but he still lies. He's willing to let his conscience bother him and to take the chance of being found out in order to gain whatever advantage lying seems to offer.

Since most kids do feel twinges of conscience about lying by this age, why do they do it?

Sometimes they simply do it to "feel big." A youngster will brag or tell tall tales to get admiration or acceptance, and the "big shot" feedback is so pleasant, it dwarfs the tiny prick of conscience. This kind of lying isn't very serious and sometimes you can ignore it unless it's a regular occurrence. But what about another kind of lying—the kind that happens because the child *fears the consequences of telling the truth?*

It's hard to take your punishment like a man (as even girls are told to do) if you're a quite young person. It's pretty tempting to avoid punishment by lying. So you get the kid who swears up and down that she wasn't the one who lost the bracelet, forgot to walk the dog, etc. You can't let this kind of lying go. But what's the best way to handle it? One way is to look at the whole child for reasons why it's happening. One parent put it this way:

> I couldn't understand why Larry was so truthful and Sam, our younger boy, lied so often. We thought we'd treated them both the same. What we finally realized was that Larry was a lot tougher than Sam. He could take our yelling and even an occasional spanking if he did something wrong. But Sam was crushed by controversy. He couldn't handle our disapproval. He'd do anything to avoid a scene, including lying. We finally decided that if we wanted Sam to stop lying, we had to make it easier for him to tell the truth by curbing our style of "scream and make up."

There's another aspect to lying and that is that it's a good idea not to force your child into situations where he'll have to lie to save face.

For instance, if you know for sure that it's young Mark who broke those basement tiles, don't ask him who did it. Just say, "Listen, Mark, I'm really annoyed that you broke those tiles downstairs. I told you not to play golf on that floor. Now you have to spend the weekend helping dad replace those broken tiles."

When your child lies, confront it. "I want the truth. I really hate it when you lie to me." These are legitimate statements. If you want an end to the lying, you'd better negotiate. Even as simple as, "It will always go easier on you if you tell me the truth, because I value it."

The Bottom Line

Do: Catch lies of substance (as distinguished from occasional tall tales) and bring them to the child's attention. "I don't think you're telling me the whole story about this, Jason."

Do: Make sure you're in the right if you accuse a child of not telling the truth.

Do: Try to be truthful yourself, and provide a good model.

Don't: Design such harsh punishments that the child is forced to lie to escape them.

Don't: Say you won't punish if he'll only tell the truth, and then go back on your word.

Money

Ride a cock horse
To Banbury Cross
To see what Tommy can buy;
A penny white loaf,
A penny white cake,
And a two-penny apple pie.

Money matters are not unknown among the young. How to get it, how to spend it, whether to save it—all are concerns of six-, seven-, and eight-year-olds.

In these primary years, kids begin to learn the power of money. And sometimes power corrupts. You may find that your second-grader who went to school with milk money is spending his wad on candy. Or that your six-year-old loses his lunch money with unflagging regularity.

Some kids spend everything they've got immediately. Others are so intrigued by the idea of having money that they stash it, finger it lovingly, and are reluctant to part with it for anything. They ask *you* to buy what they want so they can save their own money!

Getting to be responsible with money is a long, slow process. Ask anyone who has ever tried to stick to a budget. Parents need to provide clear guidelines about money and be good role models of fiscal responsibility themselves. Whether you have a child who is a tightwad or a spendthrift, you'll find that you need to lay down some basic rules on the wise use of money now, while allowance amounts are still small.

Up front is the best way to deal with money discussions. Now's the time to talk about the value of a dollar and about your own family situation. There's nothing wrong with explaining to your youngster that your family lives on a modest scale. There's nothing wrong with telling her what things cost. If you're concerned about the budget, your child probably already senses that. Why pretend that money doesn't matter?

Keep the chat about funds friendly, brief, and general. *Not* heavy. It doesn't make sense to burden a child with worries about how the next MasterCharge bill is going to be paid. On the other hand, if dad is out of a job, you shouldn't pretend to Cindy that nothing's wrong and promise her that she can still go to summer camp. That's keeping your child out of touch with reality. What's more, most kids resent it (even six-year-olds!).

There's no reason why money discipline can't be handled in a reasonable and cooperative way. It's one way to demonstrate to your youngster that you think she's growing up and is a participating member of the family. Tackle the subject of budgeting positively. "If we can save some money on the utility bill this month, we can all go to the ice show." Or, "Did you know that every time you turn the lights off when you leave a room it saves us some money?"

You can certainly suggest that your youngster limit his material demands as a form of budgeting. Don't be coerced or conned into buying too many material things for your children. And never be afraid to say that you think something is unnecessary or expendable.

Watch out that, as a parent, you don't buy your child something for the wrong reasons. Ask yourself, "Am I buying this to feed my own ego, or so the neighbors will see I'm successful, or because I'm trying to buy my kid's affection?"

One way to educate your child about money matters may be to start giving a small weekly allowance. Make the amount small; you don't want him practicing his budgeting with megabucks. Explain that the money can be spent or saved. And if his allowance doesn't last the week, don't advance him part of next week's. You're trying to teach him money discipline.

At first, you may have to exert some authority over what the money is spent on. If there are some purchases that are against the rules in your home, then you should tell the child beforehand what they are. If you're against buying war toys or toy guns, then obviously he can't buy them, even with his own money. If you have a policy on candy, then you'll have to spell it out. Don't say, "You can buy anything you want," unless you're prepared for twenty-five packets of bubble gum.

Decide how far you're willing to go to let your child make mistakes of judgment, because how you spend money is one area where experience seems to be the best teacher. There's no more dramatic learning experience than depriving yourself of seven weeks of treats and then finding out that the toy you saved up for wasn't worth it.

Money is certainly a stress point in many households. Sometimes it's hard for parents not to vent their money problems on their children. It's a fact of life that the cost of a child's upbringing has increased dramatically. But as a parent you have to keep in mind that your six-year-old didn't ask to be born in an age of inflation. The trick is to be realistic, without being hysterical, about money matters.

The Bottom Line

Do: Begin to give a primary-grader money responsibilities.

Do: Develop intelligent choices of where to spend and where to save.

Do: Explain how money is budgeted in your house.

Don't: Give too much too soon.

Don't: Cry poor mouth.

Don't: Deliver the message that you feel your children are not "cost effective."

Don't: Criticize or make fun of a child's choices of handling money.

Stealing

> *Charley, Charley,*
> *Stole the barley*
> *Out of the baker's shop.*
> *The baker came out*
> *And gave him a clout*
> *Which made poor Charley hop.*

Many children of six, seven, and eight suddenly develop "light fingers." They will swipe a friend's transistor radio, the school magnet, or even steal coins from mom's purse. A parent may be horrified to discover that a bright, charming, well-behaved girl or boy is a petty thief.

What does it mean when a child of this age steals? Usually, it means that "I want" or "I need" is stronger than the child's newly developed moral strength. Sometimes it's a way of showing off to other kids. And sometimes it's simply an experiment. "Let's see what happens if . . ."

Fortunately, children of this age are pretty bad at stealing and an alert parent or teacher can usually solve the case. In one classroom, several items disappeared suddenly. The teacher announced that they were missing and that the class really needed them back. She suggested that if anyone happened to "find" any of them, the class would appreciate their return. The next day a seven-year-old came in with a pillowcase full of the missing items. "Look what I found at home," he announced.

The important thing about the discipline of stealing is to hold the child accountable. You don't have to be Sherlock Holmes to figure out that if a radio suddenly appears in young Jack's room, there's a good chance he swiped it. And if he says, "Jimmy gave it to me," you'd better check out his story. The same thing holds if you find that your youngster is suddenly a big spender or if you suddenly find a cache of cash in Joan's jeans. You'll have to follow the clues, even if they lead to your purse.

If you're sure you've got an airtight case, justice should be swift. The stolen item must be returned immediately to its owner, with the proper apology. To be caught red-handed and have to face the music by apologizing to the person you stole from is usually enough to make a day to remember for most young thieves.

I remember once my little brother and a friend took some candy from the corner grocery store at about this age. It was not exactly the Brink's heist. But still, the boys were marched back to the store and forced to confess. The disgrace permeated our house for days. The point is, my family still remembers the incident. I assure you, neither of those boys ever stole again.

Sometimes it's a good idea to both discipline the act and remove temptation. If mom's purse or dad's wallet seems to be an irresistible lure, keep them out of reach for a while, until your youngster can control himself. Put your guests' handbags out of reach too, or you may be sorry.

Don't be an extremist. If you should get a call from school about your child stealing, don't let your embarrassment or horror lead you to overreact. Your child is *not* a candidate for reform school because she took a box of crayons. Yes, she needs to be disciplined. But whipping, or other severe physical abuse, won't beat it out of her. In fact, it may have just the opposite effect.

The other extremes can be just as bad. Sometimes a parent refuses to believe a child is stealing, even though the evidence is all around. Don't make excuses if the school calls. Don't assume that the other kid did it, or that young Raffles is getting a bum rap. Keep an open mind and a locked jewelry drawer and discipline with both firmness and compassion.

Certainly stealing is behavior you want to discipline. And

you want to keep an eye on it. If stealing becomes chronic, then something else is operating and you'll have to take a closer look at the "why."

The Bottom Line

Do: Be aware that your child may try stealing, once or several times.

Do: Deal with stealing swiftly and consistently, as soon as you discover it.

Do: Make your youngster accountable to the person he or she stole from.

Do: Talk about stealing. Stress the family value that stealing is unacceptable.

Don't: Pretend that it isn't happening.

Don't: Blame someone else (the school, bad company, former spouse, yourself). It's a waste of energy.

Don't: Make deals. ("We'll pretend this never happened if you promise never to do it again.")

Don't: Spank or punish out of all proportion to the seriousness of the "crime."

Disregard

> *Ding dong bell,*
> *Pussy's in the well;*
> *Who put her in?*
> *Little Johnny Green.*

It's certainly no secret that many adults are uneasy about the way many kids are behaving these days. *Something* is wrong, and it shows up clearly in school, even with some six-, seven-, and eight-year-olds.

What is this *something* and how is it linked to discipline? In an effort to put a finger on it, I talked with a number of parents and educators and asked them if they could identify the one thing they were most concerned with in children of today. Interestingly enough, crime and drugs and sex were not highest on the list of parent and teacher worries. Instead, I heard over and over again, *disrespect, rudeness, lack of feeling, DISREGARD.* Some of today's children don't seem to care about anything—not manners, property, ideas, adults. Not teachers, work, responsibility, or people in trouble. Not even, some parents say sadly, their loved ones. Like the tiny hero of Maurice Sendak's book, *Pierre*, these children are telling us in myriad ways, "I don't care."

In what ways does this disregard show itself? Teachers told of shoving in elevators, of vandalized bathrooms, of truancy in epidemic proportions, and of general apathy and boredom. They spoke of foul language, of rudeness to older people, and of pecking-order cruelties to other children. And all of this unlovely behavior seemed to exist as much in affluent suburbia as in the urban poverty pockets.

Parents all share a sense of shock at this new scene.

"I wouldn't have dreamed of treating my parents the way my kids treat me," said one mother. And another one said, "I see my neighbor's kids. She does everything for them and they treat her with no respect. They act like they don't even know she's their mother."

Over and over I heard the same story. Disregard. Trash the environment. Trash everything. *No caring.* As if the tap marked *fellow feeling* had been turned off.

How did we get to this place? And how can we get out of it?

The Self-ish Era

Partly, we got here on a wave that carried the whole society with it. Self-fulfillment seemed to have the accent on the *self* part. Almost every book had "self" in the title. All the advice we got dealt with looking out for Number One. Our TV ads and our TV programs all convey the message that we should "go for it," whatever "it" is. Is it any wonder that our kids have picked up on this very selfish theme and have (understandably) inferred that it means that you don't care anything about other people?

Kids who have been indulged, who have come to think of themselves as the center of the universe, are often among the "disregarding." So are the kids who have been abused or disregarded themselves.

How do kids learn to care about other people? By seeing examples of caring around them. In the "olden days" youngsters used to see a family caring for an aged relative, or someone who came over "from the other side." Every church or synagogue had its community charity work or some caring program. And disrespect was a mortal sin.

Nowadays, for many people, this model of virtue with a religious base has disappeared. If someone needs help, nursing home or therapist or welfare provides it. Families are scattered. No one's in touch. We make it on our own, without help. We're okay, and if we're not, we don't ask for help and we don't give it.

What does this say to our children? Is it any wonder that they have gotten the idea that no one else and nothing else matters but their needs and impulses? How will this manifest itself when they're grown up? How will they treat us when they're adults and we're old? What will happen when a generation of disregarders is in charge?

The Discipline of Caring

If you've asked yourself any of these questions, you'll be comforted to know that there is a discipline of caring. We *can* teach regard for others. But it needs to be a conscious thing in our homes. We need to talk and most of all to live a concern, not only for the other members of our nuclear family, but for the people down the block and even in other parts of the world.

Caring shows in all kinds of ways. In a small sense, manners are a form of caring. In the world of a six-, seven-, or eight-year-old, there's:

- Holding a door for adults
- Waiting in place in a line, instead of pushing to the front.
- Waiting until someone is finished speaking, rather than interrupting.

And, in bigger ways, there's:

- Helping a friend with homework.
- Volunteering to take your sister's paper route if she's sick.
- Setting the table or shopping if both parents are working.
- Nursing a sick pet.
- Greeting the new people who moved in down the street and helping them to feel at home.

And, in the biggest ways, there's:

- Relating to other people's needs and feelings.

· There's *empathy.* Teaching your child to stand in the other fellow's shoes once in a while. How does it feel to be physically handicapped or a minority or poor? Now's the time to talk about caring and to do something.

That's the message that has to come across from parents. If you want kids who care, you'll have to build it into family life and discipline.

Firebugs

Around this same age, some children develop a morbid fascination with fire. It's scary if you begin to see your child's eyes light up whenever someone strikes a match. Said one father, "I had always warned David not to play with matches. Now here he was at seven, unable to keep his hands off them."

Children simply don't believe in the destructive power of fire. And, of course, it does have a magic quality that's almost irresistible. How many times have you stared for hours at the burning logs in your fireplace?

So first, you have to acknowledge that a certain amount of fire fascination is normal. Now, how do you channel it so that it isn't dangerous or destructive?

The first thing to do is talk about it. You're not going to be able to squelch your young pyromaniac's interest, so you might as well work through it to find some good end. Explain how fire works—what it can do and what it can't do. You might read a book about it with your youngster. This is not to frighten your little firebug, but just to get the facts straight. Why do we light fires in closed containers? Why is it a bad idea to burn leaves in the backyard? Why is there a screen in front of the fireplace? What are smoke detectors for?

Fighting Fire with Fire

The trouble with *forbidding* your youngster to ever light a match is that he only has to break the rule once for there to be a tragedy. It's vital that you work out a strong rule that is safe and that you're quite sure won't be broken. And to tell *why.* Sometimes you can fight fire with fire. Why not say that he or she can only light a match or a fire when supervised by a grown-up? That way, if your youngster feels the urge, you'll be there to keep an eye on things. Whenever you can, let fire-lighting urges be vented in a harmless way. Ask for assistance in starting the picnic fire, or the outdoor barbecue. Let your youngster light the candles for the company dinner, with your supervision.

In a little while, the fire fascination will subside.

But if, in the meantime, you should find your youngster playing with fire in direct violation of the rules, be The Enforcer. Taking away a special privilege, "grounding" the offender for a week, even spanking if that is severe punishment in your house, all show that you mean business about this one.

The Bottom Line

Do: Understand that it's normal for children this age to find fire fascinating.

Do: Negotiate rules that are safe and that have a good chance of working.

Do: Teach your youngster safe ways of handling fire, and allow him to experiment with it under supervision.

Don't: Allow a violation of your fire rule to go unpunished. Be tough.

Don't: Ever punish a child with fire to teach a lesson.

Don't: Say one thing and do another. Make sure you follow the fire safety rules you're preaching.

TV: Taming the Tube

TV is a sore point in many households. Here are some typical complaints:

"My child watches too much TV."

"The programs aren't suitable for kids."

"There's too much sex and violence."

"My youngster doesn't read. I blame TV."

"TV interferes with outdoor play."

"My children want everything they see advertised on TV."

Sad to say, many of these complaints are justified. Much of what is offered in television programming is junk and, like junk food, doesn't provide much nourishment of any kind. Some programs are junk of another sort. They depict in graphic ways bizarre subjects that six-, seven-, and eight-year-olds are simply not ready for.

What's the solution? Chuck the TV set out the window? Get rid of it? Some parents have done just that, but it seems a rather extreme answer to the problem. Besides, it doesn't allow for the fact that the tube is not all wasteland. There are some very good programs for children, ones that can expand your child's imaginative life and add to his store of knowledge.

The trick is to take a stand. Monitor the watching. Tame the tube rather than have it control you. Because, in fact, TV is tied up with your child's school progress, emotional health, and physical well-being.

The latest statistics indicate that the average American youngster spends four hours a day in front of a television screen. Regardless of the *quality* of what they're viewing, the hard facts are that while Jack and Joan are watching TV, they can't be doing anything else. No reading. No running around. No play, no work, no study. No exercise or chores or, especially, just sitting around *thinking*!

We all know that it is hard to stop watching TV. We've all gotten "involved" and later wondered why we watched something so stupid. But if we're going to control viewing for our kids, we're going to have to first of all provide a model of a parent who doesn't OD on TV.

TV Downtime

Maybe families should have TV *downtime*—a time when the set is off for a specified period. Of course, deciding when it should be off implies decisions as to when it should be on. That's even harder.

No one can blame a parent for taking advantage of the baby-sitter qualities that TV can offer. They certainly come in handy at that busy supper hour, for instance. But should you allow the child to watch before *and* after supper? Should the watching be before homework or after homework? Should it be whenever it's convenient or, rather, when the program's worth watching?

These are the crucial questions. You'll have to make informed choices.

Many parents make rules for TV watching on school days. Some say an hour a day. Others say two hours is more realistic. It depends to some extent on your family setup. If you as a family tend to be heavy TV viewers, you can't very well have a double standard. On the other hand, if you think TV watching is starting to take over your lives, perhaps everyone in the household needs to kick the habit.

TV Togetherness

Richard Hendrick, who teaches a course called "Children and Television" at Dartmouth, thinks it's a good idea for parents and children to watch programs together. That way, they can talk about them and put certain things they see into perspective. Commercials, for instance. Children in the primary grades sometimes have a hard time separating ads from drama. If the man on the tube says, "Tell your mom to get you a Wonderfun Electronic Toy today," your child may take it as a directive from a teacher. And you're going to have some explaining to do if you haven't briefed your offspring about commercials.

Most educators agree that parents should monitor both the quantity and the quality of what their kids watch. You may be able to keep half an eye on the tube while you're making the salad, but you should also take the time to sit down with your children occasionally and watch what they're watching. You may be shocked.

Recently, a group of parents who took the trouble to watch TV did something as a result. They took the TV set out of the family room and put it in a closet. It is now brought out only for special programs which the whole family can watch together. Admittedly, this is a rather drastic form of TV discipline. But it's one way to tame the tube.

Enforcing TV rules works better if you do it in a positive way. "Hey, Pam, there's something terrific on Disney today. It's about horses." Or, "Roger, you may want to skip cartoons on Saturday morning and save your time for the two-hour special space movie." If you encourage children to watch good things and to make choices, you'll be helping them to become critics.

Rules for the Tube

Kids, like adults, go on TV binges once in a while. If your child is home from school sick, or stuck in the house because of the weather, a little more TV than usual is understandable. But don't be afraid to absolutely nix a program that you feel is unsuitable. Programs where the main theme is always violence, and programs that focus on explicit sex are not suitable viewing fare for children of six, seven, and eight. Certain subjects affect some children more than others. If your youngster has nightmares or behaves in an unusual manner after watching a particular show, you should try to figure out what it is about the program that triggers the behavior.

One of our sons used to watch Popeye every evening. It was full of cartoon characters socking one another. My husband usually came home from work about the time that the cartoon ended. We noticed that Mark began to greet his father with a swinging roundhouse punch. Poor dad was nonplused; he deserved better. We finally made the connection between the hitting and Popeye's punches. Soon after we switched channels, the hitting stopped.

The Bottom Line

Do: Watch the TV watchers. Be conscious of what your kids are seeing and how often they see it.

Do: Make it clear to your kids what values you hold dear, and take the time to discuss TV content that enhances or violates those values.

Do: Be a good model.

Do: Establish sensible rules. Monitor both time and content. Some programs are not for children. Use your good judgment.

Do: Insist that chores and homework not be neglected in favor of TV.

Do: Be flexible. If there's something special on, give the kid a break.

Don't: Use TV as a bribe or punishment. It gives it too much importance. If you say, "Because you did that, you can't watch TV for a week," you're making TV into a big treat.

Don't: Slip into sloppy viewing habits yourself. Check out how many hours a day you watch!

S-E-X Again

Georgie, Porgie, pudding and pie,
Kissed the girls and made them cry.
When the boys came out to play,
Georgie, Porgie ran away.

It's difficult for many parents to find a comfortable way to deal with their children's sexuality. Mom and dad usually accept the fact that children have sex drives. What many of them can't handle is seeing them in action. Even liberated parents find it difficult to listen to the mattress squeaking in the youngster's room if they know that it signals that the child is masturbating. A couple may be proud of their bright and precocious eight-year-old, but when they happen on the same child and her girlfriend "practicing" making love by lying on top of each other nude, they are appalled. Even angry.

It gets harder to deal with sex as your child gets older. Eight-year-old David may have been pleasuring himself since he was two. But what was only child's play a few years ago may, at this age, seem upsetting. In addition, parents worry about the common sex play that goes on boy to boy or girl to girl. They may wonder if it foreshadows homosexuality. They may be concerned because a daughter or a son is, for a little while, voraciously interested in sex (girls come in for more of this kind of worry than boys). They wonder if their offspring is headed for a life of promiscuity.

These are some of the things parents worry about. Most of these concerns, you'll be happy to hear, are unnecessary. Sex play has always been and probably will always be a part of growing up. Kids have been playing doctor for generations. Children masturbate. They tell dirty jokes. They undress each other and compare and look and touch. They experiment with members of their own sex and members of the opposite sex. Playing around at the edges of sex is the way in which children prepare themselves for the adult responsibilities of their own sexuality. If you cut off this experimentation altogether, by punishing or frightening it away, you may drive these powerful urges underground, only to have them surface later in ways that are far less healthy.

Setting Limits

On the other hand, you must set limits. A responsible parent can't allow a six-, seven-, or eight-year-old complete freedom in any area, and certainly not in one where society has such clear taboos. Sex, like other impulses, needs discipline appropriate to the age of the child and the culture of the neighborhood. Beyond this, whose feelings do you discipline, yours or theirs?

Probably a little of both.

Some general limits seem reasonable. Take the subject of masturbation. Can you forbid it? On what grounds? You can't say it's unhealthy, because that isn't true. You could say that you find it disgusting, but that delivers the message that sex urges aren't nice. What you can probably most safely say is that it is a private activity, and must be done in private. Other than that, you're going to have a difficult time explaining why your youngster should stop doing something that feels so good.

Sometimes the community you live in has a great deal to do with the way in which you approach the subject of group sex play. One mother told us that her seven-year-old boy had been "caught" in a neighbor's backyard tree house with a seven-year-old girl. The neighbor (whose children were *not* involved) was horrified at the fact that the children were exposing themselves. For a while, it was a neighborhood issue. Both youngsters were given the status of youthful sex offenders.

The girl's mother punished her severely. The boy's mother didn't punish him, but still it was made clear to him that most people do not look with favor on small children indulging in sex play. This is a fact of life and there is no way that you can shield your child from it unless you live like hermits. So sex discipline lies in making rules that will keep your youngster from being a pariah in the real world and at the same time keep him comfortable with his own desires and curiosity. It's tricky, this sex business. Be understanding. Answer your youngster's questions with frankness and sensitivity. You should never punish or spank a child or make a big issue over sex. And if your youngster shows an inordinate amount of curiosity about your body, don't inflame it by walking around naked. Many psychologists feel that it is not good for a youngster to see parents naked when the child is struggling with his own sexual feelings. Better to get him a book on anatomy.

One thing to be reckoned with in any sex discussion is changing sex patterns in the society as a whole. Nowadays kids mature much more quickly. Girls of nine and ten wear bikinis. Both boys and girls are urged by the media to be copies, in dress and action, of older kids. In the race to grow up faster and faster, we may be bypassing certain necessary steps of sexual growing up. It's up to parents to resist this trend, not encourage it.

Another factor that may enter into children's attitudes toward sex is changing family patterns. Single parents with live-in male or female partners may invite questions from their children. The questions deserve thoughtful answers. Parents have a right to live their own lives. At the same time, they should know that children form ideas of sex from how their parents behave.

How Much Information?

On the subject of books, I'd be inclined to remove pornography from primary-graders. At this age, they're not equipped to deal with magazines like *Hustler*. You can simply say, "NO," and banish it if it should happen to come in the house.

On the other hand, you have to be ready to answer questions about sex with frankness. Be glad that your children look to you for answers, no matter how disquieting the questions are. Some kids ask questions to try to embarrass their parents. Other kids genuinely want to be straightened out on some point. (Sometimes they have very bizarre notions about the facts of life.) You can do a real service for your offspring by sitting down with her and a good book and answering questions.

Once in a while, sex gets compulsive, even among kids. If you see that your child is devoting an inordinate amount of time and effort to talking or playing sex, or if she's touching herself constantly, you should look for causes of this exaggerated interest. Overconcentration on sex is often an expression of stress or frustration. Discipline, at this point, won't make it go away. (See Stress section, p. 124.)

The Bottom Line

Do: Understand that sex play and masturbation are normal.

Do: Answer your child's questions about sex and/or provide books that answer them.

Do: Discipline your child to understand concepts of appropriate and private sex behavior.

Don't: Act revolted, embarrassed, or angry at childish sex.

Don't: Allow your youngster to read inappropriate pornography or to see X-rated cable movies. These are not children's fare!

Don't: Encourage sexy or provocative clothes or actions and then discipline the resulting behavior.

Tattling

Tattle Tale Tit
Your tongue shall be slit
And all the dogs in our town
Shall have a little bit.

Children have probably been snitching on each other since this old nursery rhyme was written down. They do it from about age six until they're ten or eleven.

Why? Many children tattle as a way of showing that they've learned the rules. They know what's right and wrong. Teachers of first-, second-, and third-graders hear lots of:

"Ms. Gardiner, Jimmy wrote his name instead of printing it."

"Mr. Rosen, Ellie didn't put her book away."

"Mrs. Charles, Sam talked when you were out of the room."

Looked at from an adult point of view, tattling isn't very attractive. But from the moral eye-level of a kid in the primary grades, it's perfectly legitimate. It puts you on the right side of things and it also can be a way of seeing what happens when someone else doesn't follow the rules. The tattler's philosophy is that it's easier to learn from someone's else's mistake than to make the mistake yourself!

Some children tattle at home to get approval. Siblings will often squeal to a parent to get into a favored position, especially if the "squealee" is perceived as getting all the approval. It's a good idea for moms and dads *not* to get too involved in this kind of tattling game. If it goes on often in your house, you might want to figure out why the tattler needs to be the good guy so much. In the hierarchy of things to work on, tattling is probably not at the top of the list. You may not like it, but it probably isn't worth a big discipline push unless it goes on for a long time or all the time. (Even in discipline, a parent has to have priorities.) Nevertheless, there are several ways in which you can give your offspring the message that you're not crazy about tale telling.

For one, you can simply ignore the tattled tidbit. That kind of action says that you don't think information that comes through these channels is worthy.

For another, you can say how you feel. "I don't like tattling." Or even, "I'm not sure that's your business, is it?"

Of course, sometimes you *have* to attend. If little sister has just flushed a diaper down the toilet and big sister informs you, this is not gossip or snitching, it's an important message!

Primary-graders tend to report everything they think is outside the rules. Where discipline comes in is to help them understand the difference between tattling and telling something that it's important for a grown-up to know. Sometimes it's not an easy distinction. But who said discipline was easy?

The Bottom Line

Do: Discourage tattling and the idea that your youngster can get special advantages from it.

Do: Discuss the ethics of "telling tales" and when it's important to tell and when not.

Don't: Reward your youngster for tattling.

When Discipline Breaks Down

Stress

Most parents of today are victims of stress. Some feel the stress of modern life—not enough time to do things, pressure on the job, money problems, moving. Other stresses are more serious—a spouse who drinks or hits, or refuses to communicate. People have problems. They're lonely or depressed. They fight. They split up. They get sick. No family can avoid all the stresses of modern life.

So it's no surprise to learn that children are under stress, too. They take on some of the tensions they feel in the adults around them. But they also have stresses of their own. They worry about things like getting good marks in school, or making Little League. They may worry about wetting their pants, or the teacher hollering, or their father hitting them, or about whether they have any friends.

Sometimes kids don't talk about these things, but that doesn't mean they're not worrying. Sometimes they misbehave under this kind of stress. And parents often punish the behavior without getting to the stress that caused it. Sometimes parents misuse discipline when they're under their own stress. Either way, stress and discipline are getting in each other's way.

It's a good idea, every once in a while, to ask yourself: *Am I being tough on this child because I had a tough day at the office or because she deserves it? Is Sally's Monday morning tummyache real or did something happen at school on Friday?*

Nipping Problems in the Bud

What happens when childhood stress becomes too much for a youngster? Or when parental problems begin to affect the whole family? Or when, for some other reason, the normal passages of childhood become skewed? The first sign you may have is that discipline breaks down. But discipline in a family can break down temporarily under normal circumstances. How do you decide whether your youngster is in the throes of normal growing pains or having a more serious problem?

Start by asking what the range of normal behavior is for your child's age and for *your individual child.* (See pp. 99–102.) Try to evaluate whether the misbehavior you're seeing is a passing phase or seems chronic. The severity of the behavior, plus the time it lasts, may be your best clues as to whether you're seeing growing pains or a growing problem.

Go to the child for some answers. If your youngster is upset, try to figure out why. Ask. Be direct. Pay attention to what he says and doesn't say. Give him the feeling you'll be understanding, whatever he tells you. Otherwise, he may be afraid to say what's eating him.

Sometimes an interview with the teacher can shed some light on blues or bad temper. There may be a problem at school that can be cleared up by some diplomatic discussion.

Above all, don't panic. Most behavior problems can be solved, if they're taken care of early.

If you have the gut feeling that something is wrong, check these warning signs:

- uncontrollable temper tantrums, hostility, destructive behavior
- inability to control bladder or bowels
- loss of appetite, listlessness, withdrawal
- unexplained tears and frequent depressed moods
- compulsive sex play
- hyperactivity and inability to concentrate

• reports of misbehavior and inattention from school
• anticipation of dire events

If your child of six, seven, or eight is showing any of these signs, it's time to do something about it.

The First Step

Your first step should be to visit your local family doctor or health center. Never assume a psychological problem before you take your child for a physical checkup. The newest medical research shows that many so-called emotional problems—listlessness, hyperactivity, hostility—can have their roots in physical ailments.

A *thorough* checkup should include a complete blood test. Often a blood workup will reveal nutritional deficiencies that may be causing your youngster's problems. Needless to say, you should tell your doctor why you want the tests done so he or she will know what to look for.

Only after you've thoroughly investigated physical causes should you consider counseling. But if all the signs point to emotional causes, you shouldn't hesitate to get help. There's no point trying to use discipline if emotional disturbance exists. You'll only make things worse. There is also no point in blaming yourself or your spouse, the child or your circumstances, whatever they may be. The best thing to do is to get to work on the problem. There are all degrees of problems. See where yours is on the scale and how dire it is.

More and more families are beginning to realize that psychological counseling is not a tool of last resort but a way to cope with problems before they get too hard to handle. And there are community services where you can get help on a fee scale that is based on your income. No one should opt for do-it-yourself therapy because they can't afford professional help. Nor should you ignore or try to forget about what you perceive as a problem child. Parents usually know if something is wrong. Neglected problems can only get worse. And they will be much more expensive later on.

Punishment, Reward, or ... ?

Punishment is what you use when rules are broken and when other forms of discipline don't seem to be working. But *when* and *how much* changes with a child's age. The parent who wouldn't think of punishing a three-year-old feels that a six- or seven-year-old should know better. Mom and dad talk things over and, at a certain age, they decide they've been too soft. It's time to crack down.

If you have the feeling that you haven't been tough enough, maybe it's time to take another look at what punishment is supposed to accomplish and whether or not other ways may be as effective.

First of all, you have to understand that you can't use punishment too often. If you do, it will lose its effect. The child who is spanked often gets used to it (or he puts a board in his pants). The child who is always being sent to her room or yelled at or told that she's bad may put a psychological board where it hurts. After a while, you won't be able to get through to her.

Sometimes it's very much worth it to be selective about what you discipline with punishment. Save it for things that really matter. Have a scale of priorities that makes sense. Using the wrong silverware isn't as important as stealing. And hurting someone is (at this age) much more serious than forgetting to wipe your feet.

Keep in mind that one of the best tools for getting good behavior is still reward. What Gertrude Stein once said about writers is equally true of children . . . the three things they need most are praise, praise, and praise. Most children will want to continue doing what they get genuinely rewarded for.

Does "reward" mean money? Or a bike? No. It means a form of sincere reinforcement, delivered in terms that mean something to the youngster.

It can be a word or two:

"You really did a good job of washing that car. It was a big help to me that you did that."

It can be a tangible reward:

"You've been taking the dog on walks all week. How about a vacation? I'll take him this weekend."

One of the most challenging aspects of discipline in the middle years is the child's widening horizons. The preschooler got out more than the toddler, but your middle-years child is *really* out there, being assaulted by a succession of stimuli and an often confusing mix of values and standards.

He may meet kids whose backgrounds are completely different from his. He may come home one day and announce that Jed said that people don't go to heaven, they get put in the ground. Or that Sherri says Jews are bad. Your child will have to cope with hundreds of ideas, some of which are the opposite of what he's learned at your knee. Some of it he'll work out on his own. Some of it you'll have to help him with. Sorting out *values* will be a big part of his life from now on, as he moves toward increasing self-discipline in the nine-to-twelve *values* years.

Chapter 7

Nine to Twelve: Values Years

Birds of a feather flock together
And so will pigs and swine;
Rats and mice will have their choice,
And so will I have mine.

What Are They Like?

By now you must have realized that this child you're raising is one of a kind. And a pretty complicated individual at that: unique, with individual tastes and quirks and style, even though she shares many of the traits common to all children.

Some of her style you think is terrific. Others aspects of it don't particularly thrill you. But you recognize that this young personality is still in a state of flux, still amenable to change. So you compliment and reinforce what you think is worthy. And you speak up strongly about the areas you don't like. Point is, you haven't stopped building character. Your discipline machinery is still in service, although you will have to do a bit of retooling for ages nine to twelve. The techniques that worked in the beginning of the middle years now have to be modified. As your youngster changes, you'll link your discipline strategies to her ever-emerging personhood. Babyish punishments won't work on the youngster who is nearing puberty. And basic rules and regulations need, by this age, to be understood and followed, even if you're not around. In short, a certain amount of previous discipline had better be built in by this age, so that it works whether you're there as watchdog or not.

What's it like, discipline-wise, living with a nine- to twelve-year-old? *Fun. A surprise a minute. Revealing. Uneven.* That's what parents say.

For one thing, some kids, like Peter Pan, don't want to grow up. Peter, if you remember, considered growing up "awfuller" than anything he could think of. Some nine-to-twelves may agree, at least part of the time. They may hesitate to put their toes into the unfamiliar waters of preadolescence. They may hang back a bit, and have periods of shyness, loneliness, and fear—especially about new experiences, like going away to camp. These situations can be more difficult for sensitive and shy kids, and discipline in the form of loving support coupled with gentle insistence can help your youngster over the hurdles and out into the world more.

By contrast, some nine-to-twelves seem to be hurtling toward adulthood. If you have this kind of child, you may see a sudden spurt of interest in appearance, much effort to break away from parental restriction, lots of attempts to try feats of derring-do. With this child you'll want to put the brakes on some of this bravado and grandiosity without discouraging the very real and necessary self-confidence that it stems from.

Most children will exhibit both sides of this nine-to-twelve coin. Their growth—and they'll do lots of it during these years—won't go in a straight line. It will be more of a zigzag path, with some hanging back, some forging ahead, lots of false starts and frequent lapses into what you may consider maddeningly "babyish" behavior.

It's a new age, with some new problems and some old familiar ones surfacing in new ways. Let's take a look.

School and Home

> *Multiplication is vexation,*
> *Division is as bad;*
> *The rule of three perplexes me,*
> *And practice drives me mad.*

Between regular attendance, after-school programs, and homework, school now occupies the major chunk of your child's day. It's tempting to drop into the school's lap the major responsibility for discipline. Don't. Unless you're prepared to abdicate entirely your guidance role, you'd better keep in touch with what's going on, including negative signals from the big red schoolhouse complex.

Sometimes the signals will surface in the form of complaints.

"That teacher is horrible."

"The work is too hard."

"Too much homework."

"I'm bored."

Many children complain bitterly that "You never listen to me." And, in fact, it may be a legitimate beef. Parents should listen to griping. This doesn't mean that they have to necessarily act on it. Sometimes it's just a matter of time before the gripes fade without mom's or dad's intervention. The beginning of a school year may provoke an extra heavy dose. Whatever the timing, it's important to sort out the serious from the not-so-serious. Discipline may sometimes be served best by helping a youngster to deal with a problem on his own.

If Jack or Joan is having learning or discipline problems, you may hear about them first from the school rather than from your offspring. It's still a good idea to hear both school and child's version of what's happening before you determine what's to be done. And it's important to support the school and teacher *strongly* when the occasion warrants. It is possible, however, that an individual teacher or even a school system could be wrong in a given situation. If, after evaluating the whole picture fairly, you feel that your child is in the right, you must give your youngster your support.

The Junior High Jungle

One milestone that can be hard for many kids to handle is entering junior high school. Often, it's a case of going from a relatively small school into a gigantic district school of several thousand pupils. Jack and Joan may now have to adjust to the teaching styles of several teachers rather than just one. They may have to travel from room to room in what may seem to them an enormous, frightening maze.

Some elementary schools prepare youngsters for the junior high jungle by giving them maps. But parents can take a hand in the preparing for junior high, too. One discipline you can teach is self-reliance. For instance, you can see to it that Joan begins to solo by allowing her to negotiate a local flea market or county fair on her own. Or how about arranging to meet at a certain time at a suburban shopping mall? A number of these preplanned expeditions can be good practice for getting around in the corridors of junior high.

Since self-discipline is what you're aiming for in the long run, you'll have to take a back seat even more often when your son or daughter hits junior high. Most youngsters at this age hate their parents to go to bat for them in school matters, so it's a good idea to keep a low profile unless you absolutely have to step in. And if you have to intervene, make sure you discuss it with your offspring in advance. Don't just take over.

Teasing

One of the most unpleasant situations that kids face when they start junior high is bullying by older children. Some youngsters get picked on more than others. What should a parent do?

Be supportive. But try not to interfere too often or too strenuously unless someone is getting hurt. Sometimes parents have to exercise restraint by not getting involved with kid fights. Keep in mind that your kid is getting closer to the time when he'll have to manage certain crises on his own. Give him some practice and some room to prove himself.

Truancy

> *Three children sliding on the ice*
> *Upon a summer's day.*
> *As it fell out they all fell in,*
> *The rest they ran away.*
> *O had these children been in school*
> *Or sliding on dry ground,*
> *Ten thousand pounds to one penny*
> *They had not all been drowned.*

Truancy is a serious discipline problem. And it seems to be growing. In some communities, truancy is running over 30 percent, even in elementary school.

Some educators blame the latchkey culture. Certainly an empty house does make it easier to play hookey from school. However, working parents shouldn't think of truancy as either inevitable or unavoidable.

Truants usually give warnings before they act. If your youngster constantly talks about hating school, has a pattern of getting sick on Monday mornings, or is threatening to quit school as soon as possible, these are signals.

The first course is to try to get to the root of the problem. What's the matter? Why doesn't your child want to be in school? Here are a few things to look for:

- learning problems
- fear of a certain teacher

- fear of a certain child or group of children
- home crises—divorce, death, family arguments

Any one or a combination of several of the above can trigger truancy.

You may feel that what your child is worrying about isn't serious. But keep in mind that it's serious to her. Some of her problems may be real, and require real working out. If they involve something you as a parent have done, or are responsible for, you'll have to deal with that honestly and in the best interests of the child.

However, in no case can the problem be an excuse for truancy. There are no two ways about truancy. It's unacceptable. School is a must. Now, this doesn't mean that you have to come down like a ton of bricks for one "cut." Most kids try an illegal day away from school at least *once* in their school careers. Once is an experiment. And while you can't really approve, it's not a federal offense. But truancy as a habit is really bad news. You have to insist that whatever the problems, you're not going to permit truancy to add to them.

Achievement and Pressure

One for the money,
Two for the show,
Three to get ready
And four to go.

Who doesn't want achievement, personally as well as for their children? Certainly it's a common value in most societies, this business of proving oneself in some way. The very fact that in our educational system we identify and track both over- and underachievers indicates that we set great store by achieving, especially the right amount of it.

What's the "right" amount? How much can a parent do to help a child achieve? And when does a parent's help become pressure?

Kids Under Pressure

Barry was not a star in Little League, but he enjoyed the games. That is, he did until his dad started coaching from the sidelines. Then Barry found that he couldn't do anything right. And the more he flubbed, the more his father fumed. One day when Barry missed a high fly, his father yelled furiously from the stands, "Wait until I get you home!" Barry was scared, and he had to do something to protect himself. So he faked a limp and told his father he'd twisted his ankle and that was the reason for the error.

But it's Barry's father who is making the error: He's way off base in the way he's pressuring Barry.

As children get older, they come under increasing pressure to achieve. Some of the pressure may come from the ballfield. Or at summer camp. Or at music lessons. But the main thrust comes from school. Oddly, it's not the kids who are superbright nor the ones who are most inept who feel it most keenly. It's the great majority—the average youngster who does pretty well. Maybe even as well as he can. It's this boy or girl who is often pressured to do better, to achieve more. As one youngster said, with questionable grammar but much feeling, "Everybody wants me to outstand."

Let's face it. Most children do not "outstand." In fact, one half of American kids are below average, either in height or scholastically. But they do what they can. They go to school and they learn. They play ball and they swim. They are dear and lovable, and hungry for praise and recognition of what they are and what they can do, not needling for what they can't do.

Can you push a youngster of this age into greater effort through discipline? Do you withhold pleasures if your youngster doesn't get all A's? How do you know whether your child is working up to potential?

Achievement may be an area where parents have to do a bit of listening and observing.

It's super to be supportive of your child's interests and skills. Sometimes encouragement is all that's needed for a child to take a giant leap forward into greater accomplishment in a skill or talent. And there are certainly times when helping your child to achieve this way is in order.

But it's also a good idea to make sure that both you and your child have the same goals. In this connection, you might want to take a look at why Jack won't take up tennis or why Joan won't practice piano. Is it because of laziness or lack of attention span? Or is it because you were thinking in terms of professional-level play and it's making them nervous? Maybe it's time to ask yourself: "Am I living with my kids or through them?" Sometimes the pressure is a social one, as in the case of the girl who gets the message that her parents' fondest dreams for her are that she be popular as well as smart.

It's certainly normal for parents to have high hopes for their children. And setting standards of achievement can be important discipline, as long as the standards are within the realm of the possible for your child. Most children will knock themselves out to prove themselves to their admiring and supportive family, as long as the space between what they can accomplish and what their family expects of them isn't too wide. If the gap is too hard for them to bridge, that's pressure. One little girl expressed it well. When asked why she was so anxious, she said, "Because I'm only reading two years above my grade level."

You also have to know your own youngster. Some kids react to pressure from parents better than others. Some kids seem to take it in stride. Other kids collapse or resist too much pressure or become depressed because of it. It's one of the ways in which individual differences show up clearly and parents should be aware of the effect they're having.

Sometimes pressure will make a youngster give up the activity altogether:

> Our older daughter is such a natural gymnast. But Betsy, our younger one, has no interest in sports at all. We feel that she should join her sister and that she can, with practice, be just as good. But whenever we take her to the gymnastic instruction class, she cries. She refuses to try.

Why push Betsy? Maybe she'd rather not compete with her sister in this way. Parents should ask: Is it important for Betsy to flip out over a back flip?

Sometimes pressure turns nice youngsters into rebels:

> Darryl's problem is school. He tests out as being a very bright youngster, but he doesn't seem to be using much of his potential except to talk back to us when we make him do schoolwork. How can we spark

Darryl to produce somewhere near what he's capable of?

It's probably a matter of degree. These parents might want to encourage Darryl to pursue in greater depth some of the things that interest him and, through those things, maybe they can get him to spend some time on the things the school wants him to do. Often kids like Darryl respond better to the carrot than to the stick. Maybe Darryl could use a little independent project.

Some children, when they can't live up to expectations, manipulate:

> When my son came home with his report card, I noticed that some of the marks had been changed. But it didn't occur to me that Kevin had done it until the teacher called me in for a conference. Knowing that I'd find out anyhow, Kevin confessed that he'd changed all the marks to "Excellent" because he felt that otherwise I'd be angry and disappointed with him.

Kevin's at the point where he'd rather switch (his grades) than fight. He sees his parents' legitimate concern and interest as pressure. Perhaps Kevin needs to hear that mom and dad respect the fact that he's trying hard in school, and that they're ready to help in any way they can. If he's doing as well as he can, perhaps Kevin's parents should praise him and take the pressure off.

Many kids just need time. At some point, these youngsters will find the activity or hobby or career that they're willing to knock themselves out for. Keep an eye on how things are going down with your particular young person. If you sense that the goals you've set for your child are out of sync with her capabilities and preferences, then better ease up on whatever—be it math drill, tennis practice, or playing the violin.

The Old College Try

Worry about college at nine, ten, and eleven? Seems a little early. Still, all indications are that college concern is moving downward. The old joke about youngsters having

Ivy League college emblems on their diapers is almost coming true.

College pressure seems to be saying to kids that the career world is a giant game of musical chairs and that there are only so many seats available. These seats go to the pushy, the aggressive, and the most achieving. Anyone else is out.

This is neither true nor fair. It gives children a very skewed idea of their own futures, particularly if they are average children, not outstanding athletes or scholars. As one mother said sadly, "Nowadays, if you're not very bright or very sportsminded, you're out of it."

We need to take a look at the cult of achievement and decide where our priorities should be. We may, by the time our children are grown, have to revise some of our notions of what is worthy. Perhaps we ought to value meaningful work in fields other than those that require college. For instance, there is a real shortage of craftsmen these days. Developing skilled hands can lead to a rich work life, and a good living. Maybe we should also be looking at college in its original lights, as a place of learning and broadening as well as a place to forge a good-paying career. And maybe we should also think in terms of helping children cultivate interests and competence in a number of areas. That way the emphasis won't be so much on *marks* and achievement scores as on true life-support systems.

A New Work Ethic

All work and no play makes Jack a dull boy;
All play and no work makes Jack a mere toy.

Once upon a time, kids of nine and up were working. Real work, in the house or on the farm or apprenticed to a craftsman to learn a trade. These youngsters were mini-adults, pushed into the work world early, with necessity dictating the terms.

We know now that those weren't the good old days. But lately, some people are beginning to suggest that it may not have been all bad, that in our zeal to restore childhood to the children, we may have overcorrected.

One such voice is that of Dr. William Stephens, a graduate of Harvard's Laboratory of Human Development. In his book *Our Children Should Be Working*, Dr. Stephens suggests

that meaningful work may be one way we can make our
children easier to live with while helping them to learn the
discipline of responsibility that they'll have to know in the
adult world.

But it's easier said than done. Where people live in more
primitive cultures, work arises as part of the natural process.
But the lives of many of us are not set up with meaningful
and sharable tasks. Training work skills in our culture
sometimes seems more artificial than organic, and requires
tremendous discipline on the part of adults as well as kids.

For many families, setting up the routines and monitoring
the follow-through seems more trouble than it's worth.
Parents tend to believe that schools should be responsible
for teaching the work ethic. Yet schools, too, complain about
the lack of work discipline among youngsters. One thing is
clear. Work discipline, or the lack of it, seems to be a sore
point with everyone, even the children.

What Parents Say about Work

- He doesn't even know how to clean his own room.
- She says none of her friends have to do chores.
- Kids of today get into trouble because they have
  too little to do.
- She won't do anything, then complains that she's
  bored.
- He said weeding the garden was too hard.
- He wants to help, but tackles jobs that are too big
  for him.

And What Kids Say

- No matter how well I do it, Dad isn't satisfied.
- They give me the jobs they hate to do.
- It's too boring to dust. I'd like to do something
  important.
- Why should I work at home for nothing? I can get
  paid for the same job down the block.

What can we make of these typical remarks from both
generations? One conclusion that's obvious is that there's
dissatisfaction on both sides. The kids are complaining about
the type of work they are assigned and what is expected of
them, the parents about the quality of the job and the
unwillingness of the workers.

So—what to do? How do you get your child to take responsibility for meaningful work? And how do you minimize the friction that arises when the discipline of work is being enforced?

The Parent as Worker

Before you insist that your youngster work a certain way or a certain amount, perhaps the first thing to do might be to take a look at yourself. Do you enjoy your own work? Do you like do-it-yourself projects, hobbies, jobs at home? Or would your general attitude toward most forms of work best be described as lukewarm? Whichever statements best describe you, chances are those feelings will rub off to some extent on your kids.

If you genuinely enjoy being productive, your enthusiasm is bound to be catching. But if you usually grouse about chores, put them off as long as possible, or act like it's all too much for you, your kids may be picking up a message you didn't mean to send—that work is a drag, that it should be avoided as much as possible. The point here is that if you want cheerful workers in your family union, it's a good idea to be cheerful yourself.

Suppose, in checking yourself out, you find that you're just the opposite. Maybe you're a workaholic. Workaholics tend to get pretty intense about work. "Don't just sit there, do something!" is their battle cry, for themselves as well as their kids. Sometimes children of workaholics become workaholics themselves. Other times, they may get completely turned off work. Neither one of these extremes is the most desirable. Still, it might be a good idea for both parent and child to accept one another's style and not get in each other's hair. Moderation is a good goal. Time for work but also time for reflection. Daydreaming can be very useful!

Getting Down to Work

To start with, you have to be convinced that your child needs to learn to work steadily and well at a given task. You, as a parent, have to believe that even if we're marching toward a world of automation and computers, individual human effort will still be a must.

One of the best ways to get your kids interested in work projects is to include them in your own. Let the kids see mom and dad doing work cheerfully and with zest. If, for instance, you're changing the oil in your car, your inquisitive nine-year-old may ask to watch or help. If you shoo her away, or tell her that she'll only get dirty hanging around, you will probably never again get a replay of that initial curiosity. But if you can take the time to explain what you're doing and share the moment as well as the grease stains, you may actually acquire a permanent assistant. Next time, perhaps, Joan can take over part of the job. And eventually, she may be able to be in charge of the oil change. Not only will this be a real help to your busy schedule, it will also be a tremendous aid to Joan when she has to take care of her own car. Work competence is the name of this game. And it extends to running a home as well as a car. It goes for cooking. And cleaning. And laundry. It extends to carpentry and marketing and outdoor work, building a budget and balancing the checkbook.

You may have already started teaching your children these skills, but now it's time that both boys and girls not only help out but take full responsibility for some jobs. Planning and cooking a complete meal, for instance, from thoughtful shopping (what's a good buy?) to cleanup afterward. Putting a wash through from first cycle to drying. Washing windows. Cleaning floors. Making minor repairs. Maybe they'll never have to do these particular chores when they grow up. But they'll have to do other things. The training helps.

"But," says the parent of a nine-year-old, "can I trust her to take on so much?"

Maybe not right away. But soon, especially if you persist.

Fair Play about Work

Work projects generally go more smoothly if the workers have had a hand in the decision-making process. (What's to be done? Who does it? Is there a time limit?) If you can, allow some choices, because ordinarily kids tend to get the dull jobs. Sometimes, of course, choice isn't possible. Then it's necessary to point out that no one in the real world does only what they want to do all the time.

Another thing—work is not a punishment. Try not to use it that way. If you say, "Because you stayed out too late, you have to mow the lawn," you're giving your youngster the wrong idea about work!

What you can say is, "The lawn needs mowing. If we let it go until Sunday, the grass will be too long. Will you do it after school or early Saturday morning?" That way you're offering some choice, while still setting some rules and a time limit.

Some work projects will not fit in so neatly with both your priorities and your youngsters'. If the baby needs watching from three to five in the afternoon, and that is your son's prime playtime, a conflict is surely going to arise. There's no simple recipe for asking your nine-to-ten-year-old to give up play for the sake of family exigencies. But sometimes it simply has to be. What you can do is acknowledge to your son or daughter that it's difficult. "I'm sorry to lay this on you, but I really need your help." Or, "I'll try to get home early to relieve you."

It's natural to have squawks, just as it's natural sometimes that you'll have to insist.

A lot of the work discipline situations can be solved with common sense. If you have a feeling for what's fair, you won't ask the impossible. For instance, to expect a youngster to give up her invitation to a party or other special event in order to wait on table for your cocktail party is obviously not fair.

And some work projects won't fit in so neatly with your own priorities. Supposing your child wants to work selling produce from the neighbor's garden? Better to let her do it than to squelch the desire for work, unless you have something much more pressing.

Follow-through

> One, two, whatever you do,
> Start it well and carry it through.

You may find that you still have to help with follow-through on some work assignments. But more and more now, you should assign some tasks as the child's total responsibility. And there should be consequences if he or she falls down on the job. For instance, supposing Jack has taken on the weekly job of weeding a neighbor's garden. You may want to help him schedule his obligation for a while, but ultimately he'll have to juggle his homework assignments and his work routine on his own. This is the age during which you have to get across the idea of continuity of work.

Try to keep the job the right size for the youngster. Often, kids want to take on adult-sized jobs with more enthusiasm than ability to carry them off. So if, for example, your nine-year-old insists on raking an acre of lawn, you'll both soon discover that she's bitten off more than she can chew. Too discouraging. Too monumental. Same thing goes for compli-cated carpentry. The best job is one that provides a chal-lenge but doesn't overwhelm. And one way to protect a kid from failure is to encourage work in pairs.

One job that many children love is helping mom or dad at the office. Filing papers, sorting letters in categories, and many other kinds of office work are made to order for nine-to twelve-year-olds. And doing them can be a real service to you. But again, scale the size of the job to the youngster's capabilities and don't expect perfection.

Working for Pay

What about paid work?

There's no reason why children should get paid for helping and cooperating in the family. On the other hand, if a young-ster tackles a job that's above and beyond the call of duty, a proper fee schedule may not be out of line. Make sure that your child understands why you're shelling out—that the pay is because it's a special job. And make sure that if there's a specific skill involved (like carpentry) the youngster knows how to do it or works with someone who does. Otherwise you'll end up disappointed and your worker will end up frustrated.

One of the money-for-work problems that frequently arises was voiced by a mother of twelve-year-old twins. "I don't give the boys allowances anymore because they make money doing chores around the neighborhood. The trouble is, now they won't shovel our driveway for nothing if they can get paid for doing it down the block."

Maybe the answer here is to restore the allowance so the twins won't be so pressed for funds. At the same time, make it clear that the family has some claim on the boys' work time because they live in a group, not because they're getting an allowance. Another alternative is to pay for some work and have this tied to the responsibility for buying clothes, or school lunches, or other things that wouldn't ordinarily come out of an allowance.

Whenever money is changing hands, there should be communication. If you promise your eleven-year-old the princely sum of ten dollars for painting the porch, take the

time to discuss where the money is going. Is he truly permitted to do anything he wants with it, including blowing it on
video games? Or does he have to put it in the bank?

These are all specifics that your family has to negotiate.
But remember, how you handle work and money affects your
youngster's work ethic.

Children of eight and up look for challenge and responsibility and independence. Parents should give it to them. And
one of the ways that you can do it is through meaningful
work, inside and outside of the house.

One word of caution: You may find that it can fuel up
family feuds at first, this work business. If you haven't
expected work before, Jack and Joan may sulk, rebel, or do
a bit of passive resistance. But your job is to press on with
your work discipline. Sooner or later it will pay off.

Last Words on Work Discipline

- Give clear instructions on how to do a job. Don't
  leave your worker to flounder, then complain that
  the job wasn't done correctly.
- Don't expect skills to come at first try. And even
  after they're learned, don't expect perfection. Do
  expect and appreciate effort geared to the skill and
  the age of the child.
- Don't use work as a punishment, unless it's a logi-
  cal consequence of misbehavior (if you spill something, you clean it up).
- Check your own work habits. Be neither a workaholic nor a goof-off, if you don't want your offspring
  to copy that pattern.
- Don't assign too heavy a load, even if your worker
  asks for it.
- Be consistent in your discipline of work. Don't ease
  up at one time and crack down at another.
- If you're paying for a job, get your money arrangements ironed out beforehand.

Peer Interaction or Peer Pressure?

How often have you heard a parent say, "He learned that
rude behavior from his friends"? Or, "She never used to do
that until she started hanging around with those girls."

Parents sometimes tend to think that most kid-to-kid influences are bad. Not so. Actually, most of children's influence on one another is good. It is comforting and reassuring to confide in a friend one's own age, and sometimes moral and ethical dilemmas respond to the "two heads are better than one" approach. Sex questions can often be mulled more comfortably with a peer than with a grown-up.

All of this is the good side of peer interaction. But it's when peer interaction becomes peer pressure that parents have to step into the picture.

Peer pressure. Here's how it works. A group decides on a code activity—for example, wearing designer jeans, painting fingernails purple, having a dirt bike, or experimenting with drugs. Having or doing the "in" things becomes the "in" group activity. "They" is the group making the rules. The child wanting to join the group is the one who feels the heat—peer pressure.

For parents, peer pressure needs a look-see from both the angle of the in-group member and the pressuree. Let's look first from the vantage point of the child who is being pressured by peers. Most youngsters from nine to twelve have a consuming need for friends and for acceptance. They want to be included in the gang, the group, the team. So rejection, whether because of looks or social standing or because you're short, studious, uncool, or uncoordinated, constitutes a form of banishment from the tribe. It hurts. Children will do practically anything to belong, especially if they don't feel particularly worthy on their own. But even kids who have supportive families and a lot of things going for them will go to incredible lengths to please their peers. Parents are often excluded from this peer club. They hear very little about what's going on in the group.

How does a parent combat this powerful force when it involves behavior or goals that go against everything the parent believes in?

How to Deal

Here are some true stories of typical peer pressure and suggestions for how to deal:

Patty

Twelve-year-old Patty is being cruelly victimized because her peers have decided that her nose is too big. Like chickens in a barnyard, the group has formed a pecking order. They're working Patty over, implying that she will get into the group only if she gets a new nose. Obviously, a nose isn't as easy to acquire as the right kind of blue jeans. Nevertheless, although they can't afford it, Patty's parents are contemplating getting her this expensive cosmetic surgery because of her upset over the harassment by her "friends."

We thought this a pretty extreme case of peer pressure. But when we talked to a group of youngsters in a similar middle-class community two thousand miles from Patty's, they indicated that very much the same thing happens there.

Every parent feels for the child in this situation. Unfortunately, if parents step in and try to deal with the group doing the harassing, it often makes it worse for the youngster. Like other forms of intimidation, peer pressure can always get to its victim behind the back of authority. Perhaps in this case her parents could point out Patty's good features— her lovely eyes, for example. Explain to her how no one is entirely satisfied with the way they look—those with curly hair want straight hair and vice versa!

In this connection, we might all profit by taking a look at the beauty code we live by. Maybe we should rebel a little bit against a culture that tells us that worthy and pretty or handsome are one and the same. Maybe we all need the discipline to look beyond mere good looks for another kind of beauty in traits we find desirable. And certainly we need to continue to give our kids the feeling that we value them for what they are, not for how they look.

Billy

Ten-year-old Billy's friends are suddenly into sampling the contents of their parents' liquor cabinets. Billy goes along because he doesn't want to be called "chicken," but he doesn't drink with the other boys. However, he does agree to play host, and afterward his parents notice the dip in the vodka level. When they accuse the housekeeper of tippling, Billy honorably comes forward. Mom and dad are shocked.

Billy's parents should give Bill points for telling the truth, and for not participating in the drinking part of the caper. On the other hand, Billy allowed himself to be pressured into taking something that didn't belong to him, and being a party to what he knew was a forbidden activity (drinking). He has to take the consequences, whether they are in the form of taking away privileges or being kept away from such "friends." A lock on the liquor cabinet would make it easier for Billy to say, "Sorry, fellas." And a good thing would be if, while Billy's parents replenish their liquor cabinet, they also help Billy replenish his self-esteem. Then maybe he won't need to break the rules in order to be accepted.

Chase
A group of youngsters decide that painting swastikas on synagogues is fun. A cop catches ten-year-old Chase in the act. His parents are deeply embarrassed and blame it on the company he keeps.

There's a clear violation of decent human values here, and no amount of peer pressure can justify doing such a rotten and dishonorable thing. Discipline is a must for this perpetrator, even if he or she is a first offender. Grounding and/or loss of certain privileges would be appropriate punishment. And certainly you should insist on retribution. Parents need to take this youngster out from under the influence of an anti-Semitic or racist gang. There's probably a distinction to be made if your child is the follower rather than the leader of this sort of thing. But it's no big distinction. At this age, children have to take responsibility for their actions, peer pressure or no.

Andrea
Andrea wants a very expensive kind of leisure outfit that has become the "in" thing. She is miserable and claims to be the outcast because she doesn't have one. After much pressure (from the group to Andrea to her folks), mom and dad finally agree to the purchase, only to discover that the expensive outfit is worn only a few times and then stuck in the back of the closet. They're more than annoyed—they're mad.

Peer pressure can cost big bucks if you allow it to grow unchecked. Discipline in this case consists in saying no, firmly and finally. Or to say that Andrea needs to earn her leisure suit by working.

It's sometimes hard for parents to sympathize with a child as a victim of peer pressure. "Why doesn't she have a mind of her own?" you cry, as you watch your child slavishly following the mob. You feel she should know better. But the reality is that even grown-ups are sometimes taken in by pressure from the group or the community. Sometimes we're torn between our own values and those of the neighborhood or the block or the country club. Sometimes, at the same time that we complain about everything our kids demand, a little part of us is proud that we can afford to give it to them. Children pick up these double signals. We have to help our kids have the discipline to withstand pressures that are harmful by giving them clear values from which to make choices.

When Your Child Is the Victimizer

It may be even harder to accept your child as the one applying the pressure. But discipline comes in here, too.

An interesting footnote to the story about Patty's nose is that she admitted having victimized other children the way she was finally victimized.

"I didn't realize how much it hurts," she said.

Discipline is not allowing your child to hurt others if you can help it. Some peer pressure goes with the nine-to-twelve territory. But if you see real damage being done, or if you overhear a phone call that spells hazing or cruelty, you must step in. You have to put a stop to it, whether your child is victim or victimizer. Look at it this way: You wouldn't allow your kid to wound someone with a knife. You can't allow him to wound with words and actions either.

But, some parents argue, by interfering aren't you shielding your child from the rigors of the real world? Naturally, you have to be selective. You have to be choosy about which pressure points you're going to confront. Since so much of what children want to do at this age is dictated by peers, if you make an issue of everything, your child may tune you out altogether. The trick is to decide which issues you'll hassle over. Purple fingernails, for instance, may be tasteless in your eyes, but the fad will fade, and on a scale of one to ten, it probably isn't worth more than a two. Truancy and cigarette smoking, on the other hand, are serious, and if your youngster is hanging around with a crowd that thinks it's smart to cut school regularly, or smoke, it becomes a discipline issue. Nine-to-twelve-year-olds do have to learn to handle some pressure from their peers. The way your child interacts with peers is an integral part of growing up. It needs to happen and much of it can be valuable. However, if your Jack or Joan is being pressured—or is pressuring others—into doing something that's dangerous or antisocial, not only should you step in, you must.

Sex and Sexuality

And why may not I love Johnny?
And why may not Johnny love me?
And why may not I love Johnny?
As well as another body?

We've already talked about children's sexuality several times. So why bring it up again here? One reason is that sex attitudes affect so large a part of human behavior that it's worth taking a look at them in every stage of a child's development. The other reason is that nine to twelve are crucial years in determining children's sexual behavior during adolescence.

How do most parents feel about sex education for their children? In a recent poll, 45 percent of the parents said they wanted sex education in all grades, from the beginning of elementary school. This probably reflects parental concern that children be prepared for adolescence and the accompanying urges and pressures.

However, there's little evidence that simply knowing how to "do it"—and even "undo it"—is the answer to the rash of teenage pregnancies, unwed mothers, venereal disease, and other sex-related cultural problems. Nor is sexual promiscuity the result of poverty, or poor education, or lack of a religious upbringing. It reaches into all kinds of homes and seems to have more to do with the times in which we live than with the neighborhood.

In the last chapter, we spoke of this societal impact on sexual values. Between nine and twelve, a parent may begin to see this value system go into action.

At the upper range of the values years, around eleven and twelve, there's lots of talk about sex. Some boys and girls begin to brag about their exploits. And some streetwise youngsters much younger can be heard telling fairly authentic-sounding tales from the bedroom.

"Making out," parents have to realize, is becoming, more and more, a subteen activity. It's not so much a question of whether Jack or Joan is sexually active. The real questions are:

- What is going on around them?
- Are they reassuring themselves about their own sexuality by "acting out"?
- How much of the sexual pressure can they withstand?
- Are they being given the information they need to make the informed choices when they are old enough to have intercourse?

The way young people deal with their emerging sexuality seems to depend not only on having facts but on having standards. And many parents are now taking another look at the standards they've been silently assenting to. Not only are they speaking up, they're demanding that their children listen up.

Dr. Mary Calderone, a noted physician who is an expert on human sexuality, suggests that children be told that not everything they *feel* like doing should be done *at that time*. Physical maturity, says Dr. Calderone, doesn't always spell emotional maturity. There's a lot of evidence to suggest that children's bodies are ready for activities that their emotional development isn't quite ready for. Rushing into sexual experiences with a mismatch of body and emotions may cause problems of sexual function later. Too much too soon may have the adult consequence of too little too late.

Parents can do their own children a service by making sex information readily available, and making themselves readily available if Jack or Joan want to ask questions, or just rap about what's going on in the group. If some of what they hear shocks them, they have to say how they feel about it. Some parents are hesitant to express their ideas for fear they'll be labeled "old-fashioned." But sex is no area to fake being a "pal." Kids are not always happy about parents' overeagerness to be open and permissive. Sometimes your youngster may be yearning for you to give reassurance that it's okay for her not to want to have a sexual relationship.

That it's not a sign that she's strange or frigid or uptight. Sometimes your son is waiting for dad to say that he, too, was scared of sex when he was younger.

We know that boys and girls mature at different times and that their sexual urges vary. Some kids may seem to be consumed with interest in sex when what they really crave is popularity. Some children mature early, but others are late bloomers. It's also human to crave tenderness and romance and commitment, as well as physical sexual gratification. Parents shouldn't hesitate to impart this idea to children as part of the teaching of a discipline of growing up.

Disciplining Drugs

Round about, round about,
Maggotty pie;
My father loves good ale
And so do I.

The New Drug Scene

The home was a stable one. The parents were loving and caring. They were horrified when they found out that their son was drinking and smoking.

We've all heard stories like this. The thing that's different about this one is that the boy was in the fourth grade. Here, then, is a whole new drug scene—alcohol, tobacco, and marijuana working their way down through elementary school, messing up the heads of kids who hardly know how to spell what they're using. The state of California reports alcohol and tobacco use as early as the second grade and marijuana use as early as grade three. A recent survey in a suburban New York high school turned up the fact that 30 percent of the youngsters on drugs had started between the ages of eleven and thirteen.

Although alcohol, tobacco, and marijuana are the drugs of choice among the young, they're by no means the only drugs in this new scene. A 1979 survey conducted by the National Institute on Drug Abuse revealed that over one-third of high school senior classes had used drugs more potent than marijuana—stimulants, depressants, inhalants, and hallucinogens—drugs with street names like School Boy and Angel Dust and Red Devil and White Lady. Things to sniff and things to snort, and drugs you shoot into your body with a hypodermic needle. But almost all had started with tobacco, alcohol, and marijuana.

Small wonder that group associations of parents, teachers, administrators, clergymen, and doctors are all trying to combat early what is clearly a major national health problem.

But the greatest threat of drugs may not be the one to physical health, although that's serious indeed. The most serious thing that drugs do is to tamper with the normal process of growing up. Just at the time when a young person is learning to cope and to become responsible, drugs can come in and wipe out success, competence, coping skills, and social relationships. Drugs don't kill the person as much as they kill the full human potential of the person, and no parent wants that to happen to a child.

Are Drugs a Discipline Problem?

We think *yes*. Anyone knowledgeable about this new drug scene has to come to the conclusion that not only do we need to have a drug discipline, but we have to do it early, before problems arise. We need to have some answers on drugs even before kids raise the questions, and certainly before they're experiencing the intense peer pressure that can propel even preadolescents into drug abuse.

Popular Myths about Drugs

The most important thing you can do for your child in regard to drug discipline is to recognize that any child can be a candidate for drug abuse. Here are some rebuttals to some of the popular myths about drugs:

- *My children are well-behaved. We have a good relationship. I don't have to worry about drugs.*
  You don't need to *worry*. But even well-behaved and loving children are curious, and drugs are one of the many things they're curious about.
- *I heard that drug and alcohol use is declining among young people.*
  On the contrary, it's going up. It's the age range that's going down.
- *Marijuana has been proven harmless. It probably should be made legal.*
  Recent studies contradict the claims that marijuana is benign. Although the last word isn't in yet

on "pot," it's safe to say that it's *not* safe. (See pp. 154–55.)

- *Parents can't do anything to influence their kids against drugs.*
  Not true. Studies of young people who don't use drugs indicate they come from close, caring families. This family support seems to play a big part in keeping youngsters from getting into drugs.

You should know that even if your children aren't experimenting with drugs now, *it's very likely that sometime they will.* There's no way you can keep them away from either drugs or the people who use them. What you can do is build into your family life a good dose of antidrug discipline—a sort of immunity vaccination against drugs.

You may have already started. If you and your children are close and loving, if you're helping your kids to develop values and giving them self-confidence, they'll be more able to withstand the pressures on them to smoke and to use other drugs.

If you haven't dealt with the subject of drugs before, you can certainly start by saying with absolute conviction that the latest research has proven *all* drugs to be harmful. Beyond this fact, you can arm yourself with the straight dope about drugs. There's also some evidence that kids who have experienced other kinds of "highs," such as those associated with intense involvement in sports or creative activities, are less apt to get involved with drugs.

Clues on Booze

Alcohol may not be illegal, but it is our number one drug problem, among adults as well as youth. It's just as capable of being abused as marijuana, cocaine, or LSD.

One of the dangers of alcohol is that it's so visible. That makes it seem more benign than it is. Among teenagers, the rate of auto accidents related to drinking is staggering. When you think of the numbers of young lives ended and crippled, you have to take a more serious look at the liquor cabinet and figure out a way to help nine-to-twelve-year-olds put alcohol in perspective.

Certainly everyone who takes a drink isn't an alcoholic. You may not indulge, and that may be a very good example for your kids. At the same time, you'll have to understand that they're going to see a lot of booze going down on the TV tube, in the movies, and in the split ranch down the block. The key words here are moderation and appropriateness. You don't have to stop having wine with dinner in order that your nine-year-old not become an alcoholic. But if you or someone in your family is habitually dependent on alcohol, you must know that it's a damaging model for a child.

As for the appropriateness part—it is simply not appropriate for youngsters to have alcohol. One thing we know about alcohol is that its physical effects are much more devastating on children. Because of their body chemistry and lower body weight, children can get hooked on liquor much more quickly than adults do. There's another thing you should know about alcohol. While many people think it's a stimulant, it's really a depressant—a narcotic. In body terms, this means that while it seems to give you a pleasant high, it slows down your muscle coordination, impairs judgment and, finally, makes you less cheerful and able to cope. It makes you feel like nothing. The cruelest thing for a child, whose great desire is competence, is to feel like nothing. If you feel like that, you use something to make you feel like something again. This is the real story behind the vicious circle of alcoholism. It can give a small person big feelings for a short time. But they don't last. A person is an alcoholic when he's willing to trade off those down feelings for the few minutes of false well-being that alcohol provides.

Forbidding drinking is probably not the answer. As we all know, forbidden fruit has a certain aura that's hard to resist. In my own family, the liquor cabinet was always available to us and, later, to our kids. As children, we were offered ceremonial wine at holidays. My grandfather made beer himself. We all helped cap the bottles and were allowed to taste. But no one drank regularly so we never thought about it much. I remember, too, that people spoke scathingly of someone who couldn't control drinking. The idea of being able to control oneself was made to seem important, as indeed it is. This may be the best way to look at alcohol.

Some parents feel they should go further. If you feel strongly that for religious, moral, or health reasons you don't want your child to touch the stuff, then that's what you should say. And that's what you should enforce.

But what if the firm words and the enforcement don't work? What should you do if you discover that your child has a drinking problem? The first thing you should do is to seek help. And it may be some comfort to know that there are a number of agencies all over the country that help families to cope with child alcohol abuse. They're listed in the Yellow Pages, or they can be contacted through a school guidance counselor. Just remember—if your child has a drinking problem, he or she needs help. And right away.

Pot-pourri

Marijuana, also called "cannabis" or "grass" or "pot," is an extraordinarily widely used drug. Its effects are still being investigated. It's usually smoked, is readily available, and most people enjoy the spaced-out feeling it provides. It alters perceptions of reality. There's nothing in marijuana itself that causes people to use other drugs as well, and most marijuana smokers don't. However, users of marijuana who get heavily involved in the drug culture are more likely to try other things.

The health facts are that marijuana smoke is more irritating to lungs and has more cancer-causing agents in it than tobacco smoke. It may interfere with hormone levels and with fertility. Like other drugs, it affects reflexes. Habitual pot smokers may become "space cadets"—they have little interest or motivation toward any goal.

Many adults smoke marijuana. (That's one of the first things your child will tell you.) But that line of reasoning shouldn't alter your firmness about your child not smoking pot.

You should tell Jack and Joan about the dangers of marijuana smoking. But keep in mind that, somewhere outside, someone will be telling them of the pleasures. It's more than possible that at some point your youngster will experiment with this drug, out of curiosity or because of peer pressure. If this should happen, and if you should find out about it or if your youngster should tell you about it, it's terribly important that you don't panic and go overboard.

One youngster said that her mother had told her that if she ever touched marijuana that she was "dead" as far as her mother was concerned and might as well leave home and not come back.

That's counterproductive for you and your youngster. If you find that your nine-to-twelve-year-old has tried marijuana, don't drive him away. Keep him close. Tell him what you know about the effects of marijuana. Tell him of your concern for his health and well-being. Don't be afraid to express disapproval of pot. You're not being square—just sensible. Above all, keep on talking and listening. This should be a time for family counsels, not banishment.

No Buts about Butts

While the rate of smoking among older people is dropping, the slack is being taken up by the younger puff addicts. All signs point to a new generation of cigarette smokers—girls as well as boys. Since the smokers are getting younger, it's likely that the ailments connected with cigarette smoking— lung cancer, heart disease, and others—will be showing up in younger populations.

It's a dismal picture, made more so by the fact that kids are smoking in spite of the educational programs against smoking in the schools and in the media. Something has to be done and there are no easy answers. Outside of not smoking yourself, you can encourage good health habits—exercise, sports participation, etc. These tend automatically to work against the smoking idea. One of the things that seems to help is constant reminder of where their parents stand. Antismoking campaigns are often won simply by saying over and over again what a bad habit smoking is. You'd better believe it.

Shaping a Drug Discipline

What you're trying to do is shape the values of your youngster about drugs so that he or she can make a responsible decision. You may need help and information for this. Drug Fair, in cooperation with the National Institute on Drug Abuse, has drawn up some sensible guidelines for approaching the subject. Here are some of them:

- understanding ("I'm sure you're under lots of pressure from your friends to use drugs.")
- self-examination ("Maybe my own smoking or drinking has had an effect.")
- firmness ("I'm not going to let you do things that are harmful.")
- supportiveness ("I'll help you say 'no' to drugs.")

You can get more information from:

> National Federation of Parents for Drug-Free Youth
> 9805 Dameron Drive
> Silver Springs MD 20902

Or you can write for the pamphlet "Straight Talk" available from:

> Drug Fair, Inc.
> 6295 Edsall Road
> Alexandria VA 22314

The important point is to keep the drug dialogue going and also to be a good listener. Often children will tell parents what other kids are doing. This is a sort of trial balloon, designed to see how you'll react. How you react—whether you're shocked, mildly disapproving, or uncaring—is what your youngster is watching to see.

If you overreact, you may lose those confidences just when they're most important. On the other hand, if you play it too cool in an effort to show your youngster that you know what goes on these days, your kid may interpret that as approval, or as not caring.

So be yourself. And be straightforward. Tell your youngster of your concern and the reasons for it. But don't expect that he or she will get the total message right away. Or even that you'll be able to deliver it without controversy. Be prepared for challenges and even back talk on this one. Kids often play with facts about drugs, even if they have no intention of playing with the drugs themselves. Challenge and debate are their ways sorting out the information. Here's some of what you may hear:

> "There's no evidence that pot is bad for you."
> "You drink. That's worse than pot."
> "Sean uses drugs and he's the smartest kid in the school."
> "All the kids do it."

What's Your Own DQ (Drug Quotient)?

Of these ploys, the one that may be hardest for you to deal with is where they point to your own use of alcohol or pot or tobacco or pills. If you're a smoker or a habitual drinker, you have to know that you're on pretty weak ground. Some parents use "Do as I say and not as I do." You can try it, but it doesn't usually work well.

It may make more sense to acknowledge your dependence and to admit that it's not desirable. Then you can go on to detail why you don't want Jack or Joan to use drugs. You might even want to use your own experience as an example.

One of the main reasons kids turn to drugs is because other kids are doing it. So it's in your interest to be in touch with other parents. Making drugs a community issue with young children can help everyone. The National Drug Federation will help you set up a group in your neighborhood.

Discipline and Drugs

The best time to discipline the use of drugs is before it starts. But sometimes, in spite of your best efforts, you find that your child is one of the thousands of experimenters. What do you do if you find the scotch bottle empty or a cache of marijuana in the room of your twelve-year-old? What do you do if your ten-year-old comes home stoned, or if you find a pack of cigarettes in her knapsack?

You can't ignore it, even if it is billed as an experiment. Now is the time to say, "This stuff is just too dangerous for me to allow it." Insist on a full family meeting with both parents and even other siblings. Try to find out the *why* behind the high. Is there some problem or crisis that led to the drugs?

It's not often that a one- or two-time experiment turns into a serious habit. Still, if you've established a punishment for drug use, you should put it into effect. Otherwise it will lose its effectiveness as a deterrent. Grounding—that is, not allowing the child to go out or have any play privileges—is one method that many parents find effective. Grounding forces the child to be close to home for a while, which encourages further family discussion. Again, you have to know your own child. For some youngsters, grounding is a source of pride, for others a terrible disgrace, and for still others, an appropriate form of "reflection time."

Habits, Bad and Not So

As children grow, they shed some habits and acquire others. Wendy may exchange thumb-sucking for nail-biting. Roger may suddenly start to blink his eyes, or stutter. Nail-munching is easier to take if you know that eight-, nine-, and ten-year-olds are the biggest nail-biters. And unless you crave perfection, it still doesn't pay to put nail-biting way up there on your list of discipline priorities, especially since peers may take care of it for you. At the upper range of the middle years, for instance, it suddenly is popular to be well-groomed, which includes having nice nails and hair. Even boys may discover that it is decidedly not "cool" to be a nail-biter. So here may be one place where peer pressure can do a positive job. In the meantime, if you want to bring up the subject of a habit, try to do it in a friendly and helpful way rather than an accusing or condemning way.

You might say, "Hey, I see you're biting your nails. Something bothering you? Any reason you might be nervous?"

You might not get a direct answer. But your question could set the wheels turning and that would be a good result. It might help your offspring to help himself.

As for stuttering and other nervous habits that suddenly appear, sometimes kids pick them up and try them for no particular reason. I remember cultivating a lisp for a while because my friend had one. Children will often imitate the speech mannerisms of a friend or schoolmate. To you, this may sound freaky. But it's also usually temporary. On the other hand, it may not be. Stuttering, eye-blinking, and other physical habits bear watching, especially if they persist. They may be a symptom of problems. In any case, punitive discipline is not the way to go with these habits. Stuttering, for example, involves a shutdown of the vocal chords. It's not under the stutterer's control. Fortunately, we now know that stuttering can be treated. There are cures for it, although punishment is definitely not one of them.

Right from Wrong

Old enough to know better? Let's hope so—at least about the big things. If your kids don't know right from wrong by now, you'd better start doing some fast talking. You'd better start saying what's right and what's wrong: complimenting when they do something decent; lowering the boom when they do something downright mean, dishonest, or antisocial.

It's crucial to continue values education with nine-to-twelve-year-olds. It's time to be straightforward about how you feel about many things—intangible ones like *compassion* and *cooperation* as well as specific ones like *honesty* and good *sportsmanship*.

The philosopher Comenius speculated that a mother passed on morals to her child through her milk. Don't count on it. Although most parents favor instruction in values and ethical behavior as part of the school curriculum, most teachers and school systems are reluctant to go too deeply into this sensitive area of moral training. So you'd better assume that you're on your own. And that your child will grow into adulthood knowing how to play the game from what he learns at home base.

At this age, your youngster will be constantly learning how the world works and how other people handle a variety of situations. Things are bound to come up.

"Mr. J. brags about cheating on his income tax."

"Mrs. B. left her husband."

"Maria's brother was caught shoplifting."

"Tommy's father says black people are lazy."

A hundred times a week, your children will raise questions on matters that involve values. They will be listening carefully to your answers.

Because you now spend less time with your children doesn't mean that they're any less aware of you or your point of view, or even that they're listening to you less intently. They hear not only what you say but what you don't say. They pay attention to what you do as well as to what you want them to do. And they are coming to an age when they can see gray areas—see laws as being made by and for people, even though they may still not be entirely ready to see "different" points of view.

Denigration: Looking Down and Putting Down

As I was going to sell my eggs,
I met a man with bandy legs;
Bandy legs and crooked toes,
I tripped up his heels and he fell on his nose.

When I was a kid, denigration, whether it was on the basis of race, sex, or any other form of exclusivity, was called "looking down your nose."

I grew up being taught that it wasn't nice to look down your nose at people. So did most of us. Yet people are still doing it—not only looking down but putting down. It's still unacceptable behavior, as it was when we were growing up. But sometimes we forget to speak to these simple home truths with our own children. So how about a little antidenigration discipline?

Putting Down

Nobody's perfect. That's why it's so easy to poke fun at other people for their size, shape, speech, sexual preference, or even their way of looking at the world.

Denigration cuts deep. And children are particularly vulnerable. You may not be able to protect your own child from being called "fat" or "skinny" or "sissy." But you can certainly point out how mindless and cruel denigration is and keep him from denigrating others.

Some parents mistakenly look at denigration as a sort of toughening-up course. "You have to learn to take it," they say. But there's little evidence that being put down makes you tougher. It may even make a child less able to cope by destroying concepts of self-image and worth. Children who are the objects of constant put-downs often find themselves living up to the name-calling. The kid called "Dummy" long enough fulfills the prophecy. If parents don't take a stand against the idea of denigration, who will?

Some kids go through a stage where they brag about being put-down artists. It's a mistake for parents to encourage this form of gaming in their children. A better contribution to good discipline might be to point out that, from the other fellow's point of view, it's not funny.

Of course, grown-ups, being more verbal, are much better at the denigration game. It's tempting, once in a while, to play being Don Rickles. But the thoughtless put-down, the wisecrack that zeroes in on someone's weak spot, is a poor example for adults to offer nines to twelves. They are particularly vulnerable to sarcasm, even though they may sometimes seem callous and smart-alecky themselves. At a time when kids are learning what to value, respect for other people is certainly something to encourage. Here are two basic ways to deal with the put-down:

  · Be supportive of your youngster if someone is

putting him or her down. Don't dismiss it. Rather, discuss it.

· If you hear your youngster denigrating anyone, explain how you feel about it and talk about the other person's feelings.

Sexism

All men are created equal. But some, it has been said, are more equal than others.

Your kids are apt to find this out before they get much older. And nowhere does it show up more strikingly than in the different treatment accorded the two sexes.

Girls are often discriminated against, even in the most enlightened families. Boys can get short-changed even in the most forward-looking school system. How does this form of put-down manifest itself? Girls of the family may have less clout in the family hierarchy. Boys may be expected to achieve more than girls. Girls may be presented with limited career options. Boys' misbehavior may be tolerated more than girls'. Teachers may discriminate against boys in the classroom and favor the girls. Girls may be asked to do more chores and to give up rights.

These are only a few of the sexist put-downs that your family should be on guard against. You don't have to be a banner-waving liberationist to support boys' and girls' equal rights and to see to it that both your son and your daughter are first-class citizens.

Sometimes it's hard to do. It's hard to throw off all that ancient folklore that tells us that females are this way and males that way. We know that there are differences between boys and girls and your children are certainly aware of them. The thing we have to do is make sure that they identify the real differences, not the phony ones.

It's time to step in with a little antisexism discipline when your Jack says, "Don't ask Joan to put the badminton set together. What do girls know?" It's also time to move in when Joan accepts the sexist stereotype and says, "I can't do this. You know girls are no good at mechanical things."

One boy told us that he felt his mother favored his sister in terms of clothes. "She'll always find money to buy her something pretty to wear, but if I ask her for something she says we can't afford it." Sibling rivalry? Or sexism? You decide.

All of these youngsters need some values discipline aimed at rooting out sexism. And in the family, everyone may profit from talking about where these false and misleading ideas come from and how to excise them from family life. Try the following points for family discussion:

- Boys (including fathers) should not be allowed to boss girls.
- Girls should not get special (pedestal) treatment because they are female.
- Both sexes should come to the aid of one another when they see discrimination on the outside. It's a good rallying point for family feeling!

Prejudice, Racism, Intolerance

Prejudice, says the dictionary, is "an unfavorable opinion formed beforehand without knowledge, thought, or reason." Prejudice directed against a certain group of people is a particularly harmful form of denigration. It can bring guilt, confusion, and cynicism to both the victim and the prejudiced person. Bad news—and certainly nothing that caring adults want to visit on children.

No one is entirely free of prejudice. What most of us hope for as our kids grow up is that they can be steered somehow toward making up their minds about people and events based on fact and their own experience. Nowhere is this more important than in the sensitive areas of how children form ethnic and racial views. But tolerance doesn't happen by itself. We need to create a discipline for it, but in order to do that parents first should take a look at where prejudice is breeding.

Neighborhood Prejudice

Most Americans live in pockets of people like themselves—enclaves of Italians, Puerto Ricans, blacks, Jews, or Irish. We live in clusters of whites, Hispanics, or blacks. Sometimes even in similar houses. In other words, we're segregated. It's no wonder that outlooks tend to be similar. And that children sometimes get the idea that the way they live is the way of the world. Not knowing how other people think or live is a direct line to fear of other groups and to intolerance. Take Emily, for instance:

Emily

Nine-year-old Emily lives in the Southwest in an all-white community. She came east to visit her aunt, who took her swimming in a local community pool. Emily was frightened when she saw black people in the pool and refused to go in the water. Emily's aunt was not able to make Emily comfortable in this situation. So what started out as a pleasant day was ruined.

Emily's parents aren't racists. They didn't teach Emily to be afraid of black people. But everyone fears what they don't know. How will Emily cope and be able to live comfortably in a city, or in college, or in the working world, or in another country? And what effect will her fears and discomfort have on black people she may meet?

Steve

Contrast Emily with Steve, whose parents have decided early on that Steve should be in touch with many different kinds of people. Steve has friends from many backgrounds. He has helped Jewish and Catholic friends celebrate their holy days and is looking forward to attending an Islamic service with a black friend.

Steve is learning to appreciate diversity by actual involvement. He already feels comfortable with many kinds of people and will probably grow up much freer of "hang ups" based on stereotypes than Emily.

What Parents Can Do

It's very important to expose children to a mix of people and experiences. Today's kids are growing up in a pluralistic world. They badly need the tools of openness and tolerance to cope with it. This is true of all children, rich or poor, black, white, brown, yellow, or red.

Getting in touch with other life-styles can take many forms, but the most important is actual contact. Children who are brought up in a multicultural atmosphere, who see and talk to and play with children of different backgrounds simply get used to liking (or disliking) people as people, rather than because of skin color or ethnic origin.

Many children inherit a cultural legacy of self-doubt and low self-esteem which is the result of generations of racism. If you are a black or Native American parent, you need to build your child's good feelings about himself, his race, and his capabilities. At the same time, it's important to discourage the notion that *only* your race is beautiful or that *all* other people are the enemy. What we're after in this discipline of tolerance is a realistic view of the world that embraces all races.

Children develop and flower through a growing sense of who they are and how valuable they are as people. If they don't develop this sense of worth they may never really be free to fulfill their potential. The worst aspect of intolerance is that it mars or obliterates these very important feelings.

And it isn't only the discriminated-against child who suffers. As in the other forms of denigration, the victimizer suffers, too. Take racism. The white child pays the price, too. Educator Kenneth Clarke points out that children may gain personal status through prejudice, but that it is unrealistic because they "are not required to evaluate themselves in terms of actual personal ability and achievement . . . The culture permits them to direct their feelings of hostility and aggression toward whole groups."

Consumerism

Shopping and purchasing wisely is an invaluable tool of competence in the world. Conversely, it's exasperating to see children waste money, nag for useless geegaws, and seem to have no sales resistance. Lack of consumer skills can cause uproar in the nicest families. Sometimes children want things and parents try to resist. But sometimes both grown-ups and children lack consumer skills. Everyone spends foolishly, and feels gypped or disappointed, which leads to frustration.

If lack of consumer skills can cause discipline problems, then teaching consumerism can help to overcome some of the frustration and annoyance. Consumerism is the discipline of informed choice.

This means teaching your youngster that all is not gold that glitters. It means teaching how to select for use and for value, how to avoid being "conned" by shoddy advertising, and how to insist on your rights when you've been "ripped off." It also means learning to live within the economic boundaries of the family income. We think consumerism even extends to the way people spend their time. For instance, you may have rules in your house about what TV programs are permissible to watch or how many hours viewing is permitted. But now your children should begin to think about whether it's "worth it" to spend "X" number of hours watching TV or whether it makes sense to spend all of a weekly allowance on video games. It's a real service to your family to teach the discipline of consumerism.

How do you do it?

- By letting your youngster help you to shop.
- By perhaps deciding to rent, instead of buy, that saxophone, at least until Jack or Joan has demonstrated a more than passing interest in playing.
- By teaching him to read labels and the small print on the toy box. (What does it mean when it says, "Batteries not included"?)
- By helping him to ask, as he reads or watches a commercial, "Is this something worthwhile or is the advertiser just trying to talk me into buying?"
- By showing your child that time is a valuable commodity, too, and that she may want to make choices about how she spends it.
- By being honest with kids about what the family budget can and cannot afford.

Parent Rights

William and Mary,
George and Anne,
Four such children
Had never a man:
They put their father
To flight and shame,
And called their brother
A shocking bad name.

Most people who believe in discipline also believe in children's rights. Children have the right to be treated with respect and kindness, and not abused. They have the right to express themselves and to disagree with parents on occasion.

Parents have rights, too. Sometimes not enough attention is paid to this vital other side of the parent-child relationship. We believe strongly in parents' rights. And we raise the issue in this age group because it's here that parents often lose them, or at least may feel them slipping away or eroding. By this time in their lives, children may have acquired the skills to manipulate their parents, by using words skillfully and by pressuring in sophisticated ways that may be hard to handle.

It's up to parents to resist knuckling under to such onslaughts. They musn't confuse a natural need for more independence with an attempt to reject parental values and guidance totally. The first need should be met; the second attempt is dangerous. Parents shouldn't allow their roles as older and more experienced persons to be eroded, mocked, or denigrated. Parents shouldn't bully children, but we feel just as strongly about children bullying parents. Parents who give in to this kind of bullying feel exploited. Instead of challenging the child directly, they may take it out on the kids in other ways that are less direct and understandable.

Disagreement between Parents

Questions of allowance, dating, school work, clothes, privileges, even religious education can all be sore points with one or the other parent. When parents disagree in front of the children, it makes it easier for parental rights to topple. Divorced parents often leave the door open to parental rights problems by vying for the child's favor and by undermining the other parent's rights. On the other hand, some single parents complain that they have all the decisions to make and they have to take all the heat. There's no one to "second the motion."

Whether you're single, divorced, or living together with your partner, what are some of the areas where parent rights get eroded? And how do you prevent it from happening?

For starters, try not to allow your kids to divide and conquer. If you and your spouse have obvious policy disagreements, work them out in private so that you can present a united front on the issue in question. At the very least, avoid making it a tug of war with the child getting pulled apart in the process.

Often, parent arguments about kid discipline aren't really about that at all. The mother who thinks dad is being too "tough" may be reacting to some *macho* attitudes that offend her in her relationship with her husband. Dad's objection to mom's coddling, on the other hand, could conceivably be jealousy. He may want a share of that tenderness himself.

All of us can bring this kind of excess baggage to parenting. To recognize it is to be a better parent. From the kids' point of view, all children will sometimes play one parent against another. It's a wise parent who doesn't try to compete with a spouse for the approval of a gaming son or daughter.

The Power Struggle

One of the commodities that children begin to struggle seriously for in these growing years is power. They will try to assert it in a number of ways. One way that usually works is misbehaving. The misbehavior can take the form of a specific act or general argument. In either case, power is the goal. It's important for parents to sense when the issue is power and react accordingly. Don't slack off on limits to show what a good guy you are. Often, Jack or Joan will almost tell you it's a kind of bargain—*you do what I want, I'll like you better.* The main reason for holding firm is that in fact you can't buy your child's respect by going down that primrose path.

Another thing—don't see yourself as a victim. The parent who says "I just don't know what I'm going to do with her" is putting up the flag of surrender at a time when the very thing your child may need most is to know that you're in charge.

The Balance of Power

Is there a balance that can be struck between the parent as tyrant and the parent as doormat? Absolutely.

Don't tolerate flagrant flouting of the family rules. It's not good for you or for your child.

Insist on your right to be treated with respect. You don't have to put up with vulgar language, insults, or rudeness in any form.

Don't let your youngster coerce you into doing or agreeing to things you don't believe in, or that you believe are dangerous or immoral.

Hold fast to your own values, rather than conforming to those you're uncomfortable with in order to be a "pal."

Do be willing to listen carefully, to weigh both sides of an issue, and to negotiate when there are genuine differences of opinion.

Breaking Away

Have you noticed that your family togetherness is starting to come apart? That Jack and Joan are often more interested in being with friends than with you? That they will pass on that lovely picnic you planned and elect instead to stay with friends?

What you're experiencing is the beginning of breaking away.

The worst part of it is that devoted parents often feel, quite suddenly, like excess baggage. Where just a year, or even six months ago, their opinions were sought and honored, they may suddenly get the feeling that their son or daughter is saying, "I can get along without you very well." Jack wants to be on his own. Joan rejects and even scorns her mother's opinion. Both of them resent parental supervision and will nag and push for more adult privileges.

What are some of the things middle-years youngsters push for?

- staying up late
- wearing more grown-up clothes or makeup
- going places alone
- having more control over their finances
- doing more grown-up activities, e.g., dating, or riding in cars with older children

Breaking away always causes a rub. But the break doesn't have to be a fracture if you and your youngster can work out sensible rules for some letting go and some holding on.

While you may see it as a challenge to your authority, another way to look at it is that some of these little skirmishes are extremely healthy. They represent a kind of testing of the waters. "Let me try this and see what happens," says the ten-year-old who asks to stay home alone when the rest of the family is going away for the weekend.

"I wonder whether I can handle this?" speculates the eleven-year-old who pushes to go to the slumber party.

Sometimes the parent will get flak precisely because the child isn't too sure of himself. Just because he pushes doesn't mean he always wants a "yes" answer. In fact, sometimes he's hoping you'll say "no." In any case, your pushy nine-, ten-, eleven-, or twelve-year-old may not be so sure as that aggressive stance would have you believe. He's still feeling his way.

The big thing to remember is that your child is still just that—a child. This breaking-away behavior may foreshadow adolescence, but it's not adolescence. Nor is she ready for adolescent experiences, just yet. Your job as a parent is to help your youngster grow in the ways that he or she is ready for, and stay a child where it's appropriate.

All-Out War

Some parents hate to give up any control over their child's activities. They feel threatened by the least little rebellion. Their objections are automatic.

"Oh, no, you don't."

"You're too young."

"Because I say so."

"I'm still the boss."

These parents meet the first attempts at breaking away head on. No wonder fractures are more apt to occur, with what started out as a skirmish turning into a full-scale war. And kids may be driven into behavior that they didn't even feel that strongly about.

The Backbend Approach

On the other hand, some parents tend to bend over backwards to accommodate a youngster. These moms and dads seem to be saying to Jack and Joan, "I won't stand in your way. I don't even know what's right or wrong for you. Go ahead."

"Yes, I see your point of view," say these folks, even when they don't. These are the parents who so want to be good guys. But they may do as much damage as if they were bad guys. Many children may interpret this approach as "not caring" on the part of their parents.

Folding

Folding is almost as bad as backbending. The "folders" start off promising to resist the pressure. They start with principles of their own. They may know that a "no" is in order. But then the pressure comes.

"Everyone else is going."

"You're the only mother who . . ."

"Just this once. Please . . ."

And there goes mom or dad, down for the count—a push-over to the pressure for breaking away.

Sure, it's easier to give in. But it makes discipline tougher later. If there is some activity which you feel strongly your child isn't ready for, better not let him do it. Parents who fold up and collapse could get stepped on!

The Elastic Approach

By far the best way to handle the beginnings of breaking away is with family discussion and fair give and take. Even better than laying down the law is making the rules together with your youngster. Often, by talking, you can get a clear sense of what all members of the family really want to do. And always, if it's a question of limits, children are much more apt to accept them if they understand that they're set because you care about them, and not merely as punishment.

Supposing you find yourself in a situation where you and young Jack or Joan are miles apart? Then you'll just have to stand pat. You're the adult and, if you have a good reason to back up your edict, you must stick with it.

"I can't allow you to go to that party because there won't be any adult supervision."

"You can't go sailing today because the water is too rough and that's dangerous."

"I think you're too young to wear clothes like that."

Once in a while, you'll want to stretch a bit to meet your venturesome youngster halfway. You may decide to rethink some of your notions about what a ten-year-old can and can't do, based not on generalities, but in light of your own special kid. Your responsible ten-year-old may be ready for solo flights before a twelve-year-old who doesn't quite have his act together.

And expect that your young adventurer may be doing a bit of stretching and then pulling back, too. One day or one month Jack may be all confidence and bluster, ready to go out alone and seek his fortune. The very next week, this same Jack may be less expansive and glad that you kept the home fires burning. An elastic approach gives you both room to expand and to snap back.

Breakaway Parents

Once in a while, it's the parents who want to break away, who can't wait for their kids to grow up or be less dependent. Sometimes it's the kids who are reluctant to leave the nest and the parents who push the child toward sleepaway camp or adult experiences.

For the single parent, it can seem even more desirable. Because it's easier. Because single parents may look on maturity as taking some of the total burden off them. Still, and even though the child may sometimes want to be grown-up, it's not a good idea to rush it. Children of twelve may look grown-up, may even talk or act grown-up at times. But believe it, they're still children. And they should be allowed to grow at their own pace.

The important message here is that too much too soon can come from the parents' side rather than the child's. Sometimes acting grown-up seems so desirable that we may rush our children into it. Being grown-up is nice, but what's the hurry?

The Bottom Line on Breaking Away

Don't take it personally when you see the first signs of breaking away. It's normal and natural.

Don't backbend, fold, or go to war if you can avoid it. Try to be elastic. Take your individual child into consideration. She may be readier to solo than other kids.

Don't rush kids into breaking away before they're ready.

Speaking Up

Sticks and stones will break my bones
But names will never hurt me.

Does Talk Hurt?

By the time the average human is eight or nine years old, she knows words and combinations of words that stagger the imagination, and parent and child are exchanging thoughts of dazzling complexity through the medium of language.

How parent and child talk to one another at any age, but particularly at this one, is an extremely important part of discipline. The point is, now both parent and child have an extraordinary ability to hurt as well as to communicate. Everyone is sometimes tempted to use wounding, wipe-out language. A parent may say:

"You never do anything right."

"I could kill you!"

"Get away from me! I can't stand you!"

We've all used phrases like this. The moment passes, the storm blows over, and we forget what we said. But the child may not. The unwitting remark may fester, getting in the way of communication long after the event. What's the moral of this story? Better maybe not to say it if it isn't worth remembering, and if you don't want to get it back.

Foul Language from Kids

But restraint on language cuts both ways. And now's the age to curb that nasty talk from children. At younger ages, you may have listened to language coming from your offspring and made excuses—lack of control, testing the limits, showing off, even mimicking grown-up behavior. But foul language, insults, and disrespectful talk directed at parents by nine-to-twelve-year-olds is totally unacceptable. You have to put a stop to it. And at the same time as you refuse to allow the behavior, you might want to ask yourself why it's happening.

Why is your child talking like that? Is it just a normal "gross-out" reflex that we're dealing with here, or is there real hostility behind it? Lots of kids think it funny to shock ma and pa with a display of vulgarity. Real hostility may indicate more deep-seated problems.

The one makes you feel annoyed, and that's reason enough to lay down the law about it. But the other gives you a really uneasy feeling that you and your child may be squaring off as adversaries. You'll have to decide which kind of foul language you're dealing with.

Whichever it is, the parent who finds himself on the receiving end of unacceptable language may find that the most effective way to stop it is to cease communication while it's going on. (This is not the same as giving a child the silent treatment for a long period of time.) You can simply say, "I

can't talk to you when you're expressing yourself that way."
Or, "There's no way we can communicate when you talk like
that. You'll have to clean up your act if you want me to listen
to you." Or it may be a good time to say, "I get the feeling
that you're mad about something. Why don't you talk about
it instead of covering it up with all those garbage words?"

It's very tempting to return back talk in kind. But it really
doesn't go anywhere when you meet your youngster at that
level. You'll have to stay out of the gutter if you're hoping to
get Jack or Joan to put a curb on the foul language.

One of the things some parents try to do is to control their
children's access to words, rather than trying to control their
use of the words. The truth is, there's no way you can keep
your nine-to-twelve-year-old from learning four-letter words.
You certainly can't keep them from hearing them in school,
or from seeing them in print. It simply doesn't work to try
to censor the books in the library, when what you object to
is written on the walls of the lavatory! You can't control your
child's environment. What you can do is help him control his
own use of language.

A good way to put it to your kids is that controlling your
mouth is a little like learning control of your bowels and
bladder. If you don't have the control by a certain age, it's
downright embarrassing—both for you and for the people
around you.

We're all tired of those four-letter words. And we're equally
tired of people saying anything they feel like saying. We're
tired of no-control, no-respect, no-holds-barred language. The
whole idea is, as the youngsters say, *old*. So when the
language gets out of hand, put your foot down.

Chapter 8

Discipline: A Last Roundup

Self-discipline

When I was a little boy
My mommy kept me in,
But now I am a great boy
I'm fit to serve the king;
I can hand a musket,
And I can smoke a pipe,
And I can kiss a bonny girl
At twelve o'clock at night.

This may be a good place to pause and look back over some of the ideas that have been presented here. What's it all leading up to? Or, as psychologists sometimes ask, what would we like to see happen?

Oddly, the ultimate goal of discipline is to be able to do away with it. What every parent should look forward to is the day when Jack and Joan are able to take over the controls themselves. In other words, *self-discipline.*

It's good to keep this end in mind. Otherwise, you might be tempted to set up a permanent control system operating from the parent corner, rather than a model of discipline that prepares kids to handle their own affairs. You *could* get too used to pulling the strings and calling the tune. Or, you could get into the habit of giving way, of not giving your youngsters any system at all to use as a model. Either of these extremes wouldn't be healthy—not for you or for your youngsters. They have to learn how to take over the reins gradually. At what age? And in what areas? Those are the subtle factors you'll be experimenting with, one way and another, from the time your children are born to the time they move out of your home for good. But do it you must. Because it's vital.

175

Self-discipline as a Survival Skill

Self-discipline is probably the greatest survival skill that you can offer your child. Lack of it can dog a person's life, interfering with relationships, marring self-image, hampering life's work and success. Conversely, with self-discipline, many other aspects of life can fall naturally and gracefully into place: learning skills, creative endeavors, friendships. Self-discipline makes it possible for human beings to release and fully explore their human potential.

Obviously, there are other factors that contribute to successful adulthood. Enough kids raised with very little discipline or with too much control do well in adulthood to provide exceptions to the rule. Still, we've been talking probabilities here. And all the literature on child rearing suggests that disciplined young adults are better equipped to face the world. Knowing this helps put things into perspective, especially when there are so many temptations to take the path of least resistance in bringing up our children.

It also helps to know that self-discipline not only has a "cost benefit" for them, but for you. How long do you want to be monitoring your children's lives? If you believe that for everything there is a season, the season for being in charge of your children's affairs probably ends sometime around ages eighteen to twenty-one.

You have a need and a right to be liberated. Parents who find that their kids depend on them too heavily, either financially or emotionally after a certain age, may wind up feeling resentful and burdened. In other words, "letting go" on the part of parents may be just as important as "breaking away" is for the youngster. If you let go knowing that the self-discipline mechanism is in place, you can relax and enjoy your grown-up son or daughter as a comrade and friend, not as an overgrown child.

Slouching Toward Self-discipline

Sometimes parents get discouraged. There's a lot of effort that goes into raising children, if you're trying to do a good job. And once in a while you don't see the fruits of your labor clearly enough.

Nevertheless, they are there. You have only to think about

what your child or children were like at two, three, and four to appreciate what time, and you, have wrought.

Take a close look at Jack. Just a few years ago, you would have had to cajole him into any new experience. Now he's raring to go and try things. He's comfortable away from home for a weekend. He doesn't need to be reminded about homework and chores. He talks up but doesn't talk back (most of the time, anyway). And Jack doesn't lie, which makes you proud indeed. He's a real straight arrow in that respect. No, he's not a paragon of virtue. At times, his room still looks like a small hurricane hit it. He forgets small politenesses when you're out in company. And he still picks on his younger siblings all too often. But on balance, Jack's heading in the right direction.

Joan is growing up, too. She is handling her feelings in a more mature way. No more temper tantrums. Sulks are few and far between. She has lots of friends and peer pressure is something she's learning how to handle. Just the other day, she said, "I don't *care* what the other kids do. They can't boss me!"

Joan is making big strides in the judgment department. You can trust her with certain decisions that you couldn't leave her with even a year ago. And she's more organized. Knows how to do a great many things. Joan's more comfortable with schoolwork now; she's finally mastered some of the math concepts that were so hard for her a few years ago. She may nag for certain clothes or privileges, but she's more reasonable about her demands and more open to discussion.

Joan, like Jack, is growing up. And while maturity is still a long way off, these two twelve-year-olds, like most youngsters this age, are slouching toward self-discipline.

Keep that in mind, as you face the onslaught of adolescence. As the glands begin to rage at your house, remember that your guidance has worked before and can continue to work, until the time when self-discipline is a reality.

The world that your youngsters will be entering will probably have in it a considerable amount of stress and uncertainty. Feel good about the fact that wise parenting can give them the tools to cope.

Ideas A to Z

> *Great A was alarmed by B's bad behavior,*
> *Because C, D, E, F denied G a favor;*
> *H had a husband with I, J, K, and L,*
> *M married Mary and taught her children to spell.*

A

Achievement is something both parents and children want. Discipline helps make achievement possible, but too much discipline can get in the way of achievement.

Approval. We all need it. Make sure that you show your kids approval when they deserve it.

Attention span. This important aspect of learning readiness begins to develop early and needs encouragement and help from parents.

B

Bed-wetting. Most children outgrow it. In the meantime, patience and understanding work better than harsh measures.

Belittling is too hurtful to be useful as a form of discipline. And don't allow your children to hurt each other by belittling either.

Behavior varies from child to child, but most children seem to go through similar stages at around the same ages. Always wait it out a bit before you decide that you've got a problem.

C

Cheating is common among six-year-olds who don't fully understand the moral aspects. As they get older, explaining *why* cheating is antisocial can be effective.

Consequences. As children grow in their capacities to grasp cause and effect, they need to learn through discipline to accept responsibility for the consequences of their actions.

Consistency is one of the most important aspects of discipline. It's confusing to a youngster if you're tough one day and lenient the next.

D

Dads can play a vital role in the bringing up of kids. More and more fathers are finding out that they can be "cuddlers" and pals as well as disciplinarians.

Delinquency is lots of little problems grown into big trouble. If your child is showing real signs of delinquent behavior, you should seek expert help.

Drug abuse is occurring among younger and younger children. Make sure your kids have the straight dope on drugs early.

E

Eating habits start early. That's why it's a good idea to make baby's feeding time pleasant and not to worry about the quantity he's eating.

Effort. When children make an effort, they should always be rewarded, not by bribes but by genuine praise.

Equal rights—do both sons and daughters have them, or is discipline sexist? All children, male and female, should get equal treatment from parents.

F

Fears are common among kids at various ages and especially common among four-year-olds. Not all fears are unhealthy, and in no case should a child be ridiculed for being afraid.

Friends become more important as a child grows. How well a child makes friends is one of the indicators of mental health, and parents can help kids with relationships.

G

Goodness can't be expected all the time. Parents need to decide whether the good behavior they're asking for is appropriate to the child's age and developmental stage.

Gripes about school are common among most kids. Some gripes disappear, but all of them deserve a listening ear.

Guidance is a must; it helps children to feel secure. Too few rules create uncertainty and may make a child think you don't care what happens to him.

H

Habits like thumb-sucking and nail-biting come and go, usually without help from parents. If a habit persists over a long period, try to figure out why it's happening before you resort to discipline strategies.

Hitting a child usually signals that all other forms of

communication have broken down. When used frequently, hitting can lead to child abuse.

Home is where children see their models for behavior and values. What *they* see is what *you* usually get.

I

Inheritance plays a part in your baby's personality, but that doesn't mean that nothing can be changed. Tender loving care can make a difficult baby easier, while neglect or harsh treatment can make an easy baby difficult.

Illness can sometimes cause symptoms that look like discipline problems. Always check out physical causes thoroughly before you decide you have a problem child.

Imagination is a vital creative source in the lives of children. It's good to encourage, not squelch it.

J

Jealousy often develops over a new baby. That's the time to show an older child that she is loved and valued, which will help her to accept the new sister or brother.

Jokes that make fun of people for their color or religion or ethnic origin should not be allowed. Children need a discipline of tolerance and parents can be positive models in this respect.

Joy is an essential ingredient in child rearing. Don't let discipline become so heavy-handed that it takes away the fun of being with your kids.

K

Kindergarten is a tremendous experience in the life of a child. Be understanding about problems that may occur as school and child adjust to each other.

Kindness is a value that needs to be taught to kids. Stress kind treatment for pets as well as people.

Kissing is one of the ways we humans demonstrate love and affection. Families that kiss, hug, and cuddle one another are more likely to produce warm and loving adults.

L

Language is intimately linked to discipline. Your tone of voice is almost as important as what you say, and parents should avoid abusive and sarcastic tones and language with their children.

Learning and discipline go hand in hand. Kids who are achievers seem to come from homes where there is firm and loving discipline.

Lying by children should always be dealt with, but the strategies vary with the age of the child. A four-year-old can't understand why lying is wrong, but a ten-year-old should be able to.

M

Manners are a form of consideration and should be woven into discipline. Parents shouldn't permit their children to be rude to them, and vice versa.

Masturbation is part of the normal sex behavior of both boys and girls. Stern discipline over harmless sex play may stop the behavior, but it may create other problems.

Money discipline should start early. Kids need to understand budgeting and be able to manage an allowance. There's no reason for parents to finance "the gimmes."

N

Nagging is not an effective form of discipline because it has a high "turn-off" factor. Kids will often ignore a nagging voice.

Natural instincts of parents can be very valuable. Believe in yourself as a parent; you know your own child better than anyone.

No is a favorite word of toddlers. Sometimes direct action is the best way to deal with a negative two-year-old who doesn't yet understand reason.

O

Obedience has to be absolute for some things—like a rule with a toddler about running into the street—but only the most authoritarian parents expect strict obedience to everything they say.

Obscenity. If your children use it and it offends you, say so. And don't use foul language yourself if you don't want your kids to use it.

Options. Parents have choices about how they raise their children, and many of them are dependent upon the match between personality of child and parent. Don't be pushed into a discipline style that you don't really approve of.

P

Peers can be a force for good or evil in children's lives. *Peer pressure* is something families should talk about.

Pressure from parents to kids often comes over school achievement or sports competition. You can encourage your child without pressuring.

Punishment is sometimes necessary. Make sure the punishment fits the "crime" and is understood by the youngster.

Q

Quarrels are inevitable, especially between siblings. Know when to ignore and when to intervene; discipline has to come in if someone is being hurt.

Questions children ask need to be answered, especially those about sex. But keep your answers simple and to the point.

Quiet time is something parents have a right to. So do kids. Give preschoolers downtime to unwind and relax.

R

Racism is a damaging trait in children and grown-ups. But often small children's innocent questions are wrongly interpreted as prejudice.

Reasoning with kids needn't mean long-winded explanations. Family rules can be negotiated on the basis of simple discussion geared to the age of the child.

Rebellion shows up at various ages, as youngsters strive for independence. Much rebellion is healthy; some requires discipline.

S

Single parents have an exceedingly tough time and may tend to have more problems with children. But the fact of divorce or separation shouldn't be an excuse for lack of discipline.

Stealing needs to be dealt with firmly. It is more serious when the child is older and understands right from wrong.

Stress is a "given" in American life. Adults who recognize their own stress should try not to burden their offspring with too much.

T

Temper tantrums are common among toddlers and even preschoolers. Long lectures don't work nearly as well as direct action to help the child put himself under control.

Toilet training is useless until after your youngster understands what a toilet is for and has learned such simple routines as how to brush her teeth and wash.

Television needs to be disciplined. Don't allow unlimited viewing, and keep an eye on the kinds of programs your child is watching.

U

Underachievers. Make sure the label is accurate before you deal with underachieving. Your child will respond more to encouragement and reinforcement than to ridicule and punishment.

Unacceptable behavior is something that needs to be spelled out for your children. But don't have too long a list or your kid may not be able to live up to your expectations.

V

Values are extremely important. Don't be surprised if your child doesn't know right from wrong unless you tell him and demonstrate (over and over again if necessary).

W

Work is a necessary discipline. Good work habits give a child enormous satisfaction and help school and many other things fall into place.

X,Y,Z

The XYZ of discipline is caring. Without caring, everything else is meaningless. But caring without discipline is chaos.

═══ *Bibliography* ═══

For every evil under the sun,
There is a remedy or there is none.
If there is one, try and find it;
If there be none, never mind it.

A Child's Journey, Julius Segal and Herbert Yahraes. McGraw-Hill, New York, 1978.

A Working Mother's Guide to Child Development, F. Philip Rice. Prentice-Hall, Englewood Cliffs, New Jersey, 1979.

Between Parent and Child, Dr. Haim G. Ginott. Macmillan, New York, 1965.

Bringing Up Children, Grace Langdon. John Day, New York, 1960.

Child Behavior, Frances L. Ilg, M.D., Louise Bates Ames, Ph.D., Sidney M. Baker, M.D. Harper & Row, New York, 1981.

Children's Views of Themselves, Association for Childhood Education International, Membership Service Bulletin 104, 1959–60.

Dealing in Discipline, Margaret Verble. University of Mid-America, Lincoln, Nebraska, 1980.

Developing Responsibility in Children, Constance J. Foster. Science Research Associates, Chicago, 1953.

Discipline without Fear, Loren Grey, Ph.D. Hawthorn Books, New York, 1974.

Dr. Gardner's Stories about the Real World, Richard A. Gardner, M.D. Avon Books, New York, 1972.

Educators' Discipline Handbook, Robert D. Ramsey. Parker Publishing, West Nyack, New York, 1981.

Effective Parents, Responsible Children, Robert Eimers and Robert Aitchison, Ph.D. McGraw-Hill, New York, 1977.

Growing with Your Children, Herbert Kohl. Little, Brown, Boston, 1978.

Parenting—A Guide for Young People, Sol Gordon and Mina McD. Wollin. Oxford Book Company, New York, 1975.

Raising a Responsible Child, Dr. Don Dinkmeyer and Gary D. McKay, M.A. Simon & Schuster, New York, 1973.

Raising Children with Love and Limits, Psyche Cattell, Ed.D. Nelson-Hall, Chicago, 1972.

Straight Talk, Drug Fair, Inc. Alexandria, Virginia, 1980.

The Child under Six, James L. Hymes, Jr. Prentice-Hall, Englewood Cliffs, New Jersey, 1963/1971.

The Complete Question and Answer Book of Child Training, Hawthorn Books, New York, 1972.

The Family Book about Sexuality, Mary S. Calderone, M.D. and Eric W. Johnson. Harper & Row, New York, 1981.

The Father's Almanac, S. Adams Sullivan. Doubleday, Garden City, 1980.

The How and Why of Discipline, Aline Auerbach. Child Study Association of America, 1957/1969.

The Hurried Child, David Elkind. Addison-Wesley, Reading, Massachusetts, 1981.

The Magic Years: Understanding and Handling the Problems of Early Childhood, Selma Fraiberg. Scribners, New York, 1959.

The New Extended Family, Ellen Galinsky and William H. Hooks. Houghton Mifflin, Boston, 1977.

The Parenting Advisor (by the Princeton Center for Infancy), Frank Caplan, general editor. Anchor Press/Doubleday, Garden City, 1976.

The Parents' Encyclopedia, Milton I. Levine, M.D., and Jean Seligmann. Crowell, New York, 1973.

The Parents' Guide to Everyday Problems of Boys and Girls, Sidney Matsner Gruenberg. Random House, New York, 1958.

The Roots of Crime, Eda Le Shan. Four Winds Press, New York, 1981.

The World of the Child, edited with an introduction by Toby Talbot. Anchor Press/Doubleday, Garden City, 1967.

Toddlers and Parents, Dr. T. Berry Brazelton. Delacorte, New York, 1974.

Toughlove, Community Services Foundation. Sellers, Pennsylvania, 1980.

Understanding Children: A Parent's Guide to Child Rearing, Richard A. Gardner, M.D. Creative Therapeutics, Cresskill, New Jersey, 1979.

What Every Child Needs, Lillian and Richard H. Peairs. Harper & Row, New York, 1974.

Your Child from Six to Twelve, U.S. Department of Health, Education, and Welfare. Office of Child Development, 1966.

Your Two-Year-Old, Louise Bates Ames and Frances L. Ilg. Dell, New York, 1980.

Your Three-Year-Old, Louise Bates Ames and Frances L. Ilg. Dell, New York, 1980.

Your Four-Year-Old, Louise Bates Ames and Frances L. Ilg. Delacorte, New York, 1976.

Your Five-Year-Old, Louise Bates Ames and Frances L. Ilg. Delacorte, New York, 1979.

Your Six-Year-Old, Louise Bates Ames and Frances L. Ilg. Delacorte, New York, 1979.

Index

About the Bank Street College of Education

Since its founding in 1916, The Bank Street College of Education has been devoted to the study of how children learn and develop, educating children, training teachers and child care specialists, and helping families. This is still Bank Street's mission in the 1980's when child care professionals the world over equate the Bank Street name with a respected, progressive, and humanistic approach to a child's education.

About the Author

Barbara Brenner is a writer, teacher, editor, and consultant to educational projects. She has written over forty books for children, including two ALA Notable Books and one selected by *School Library Journal* as "the best of the best" books for children of the last thirteen years. As a teacher, one of her principal interests has been encouraging youngsters to do their own creative writing. Mrs. Brenner has been associated with Bank Street College since 1962; she is presently associate editor there. During the past five years, she has taught a course with her illustrator-husband, Fred Brenner, at Parsons School of Design. The Brenners have two sons and live in Lords Valley, Pennsylvania.

About the Consultant

Dr. Levinger is a member of the Bank Street College of Education graduate faculty. She is also an Associate Clinical Professor of Psychiatry at Albert Einstein College of Medicine in New York. For over thirty years, Dr. Levinger has maintained a private practice in psycho-diagnostic and educational testing, and has acted as consultant to parents.